1000
AMAZING FACTS
Incredible but true facts about
EVERYTHING!

This edition published by Parragon Books Ltd in 2015

Parragon Books Ltd
Chartist House
15–17 Trim Street
Bath BA1 1HA, UK
www.parragon.com

ISBN 978-1-4723-9171-1

Printed in China

1000

AMAZING FACTS

Incredible but true facts about
EVERYTHING!

PaRragon

Bath · New York · Cologne · Melbourne · Delhi
Hong Kong · Shenzhen · Singapore · Amsterdam

WHAT'S INSIDE?

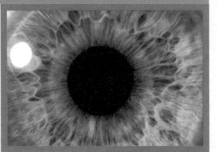

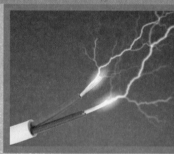

Chapter 1

AMAZING ANIMALS

AND

POTTY PLANTS

A SIX-YEAR-OLD could stand inside a HIPPO'S MOUTH when it's wide open.

#0001

The star-nosed mole has **22** tiny 'fingers' on its snout, for **touching** and feeling its way around. #0002

Ostriches' **eyes** are bigger than their **brains.** #0003

Do you **JUMP** when you get a **FRIGHT?** An **ARMADILLO** does – straight up in the air, more than a metre high. #0004

5 DEADLY ANIMALS

HIPPOS kill more people every year than sharks, bears, lions or leopards. #0005

A **GOLDEN POISON DART FROG** is so poisonous that you could die from just touching it. #0006

You can tell when a **BLUE-RINGED OCTOPUS** is about to deliver a **DEADLY BITE** – bright blue rings suddenly appear all over its body. #0007

The **BOX JELLYFISH,** the most venomous creature on Earth, is almost invisible in water. #0008

NEEDLEFISH sometimes leap out of the water and accidentally stab fishermen with their **SHARP SNOUTS.** #0009

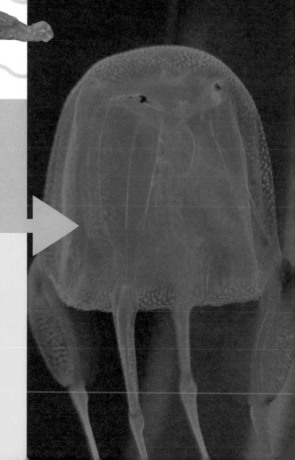

A **BOOTLACE WORM** found on a Scottish beach measured

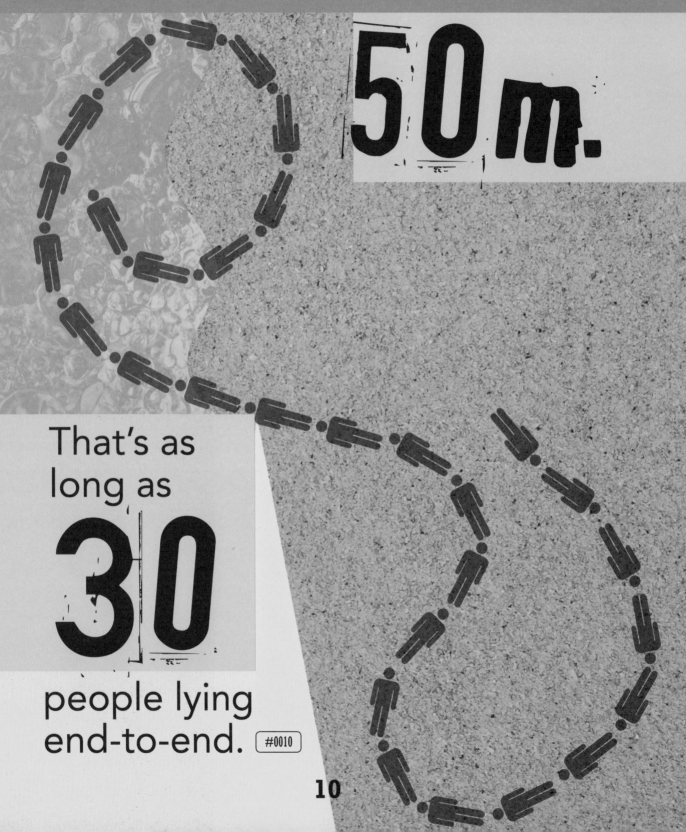

50 m.

That's as long as **30** people lying end-to-end. #0010

10 BONKERS BIRD FACTS

A **swift** can stay in the air for **over 3 years** without landing on the ground! #0011

A **bee hummingbird** weighs less than a **penny.** #0012

The **male satin bowerbird** decorates his nest with any **blue** objects he finds. #0013

The **hooded pitohui bird** has **deadly poison** in its skin and feathers. #0014

An **owl** can't move its eyes, but it can **rotate its head** to face backwards. #0015

A **bald eagle's nest** can be as big as a **garage!** #0016

Fieldfares scare off enemies by **dive-bombing** them with their **poo!** #0017

If you scare a **fulmar chick,** it can squirt fishy, oily **vomit** into your face from **3 metres away.** #0018

A **wood pigeon's** feathers weigh more than its bones. #0019

The **emperor penguin** can dive **500 metres.** That's more than the height of most skyscrapers. #0020

3 FACTS ABOUT SOMETHING FISHY...

Blobfish, which are jelly-like deep-sea fish, sit on their **eggs** until they hatch, just like chickens. #0021

FLASHLIGHT FISH have two glowing **LAMPS** on their heads. They can use them to attract food and 'talk' to each other over long distances. #0022

The **whale shark** is the **biggest** fish. It's gentle and friendly to humans! #0023

4 SAFARI SNIPPETS

Elephants use their trunks as **snorkels** when they walk or swim underwater. #0024

BLACK RHINOS have such bad **EYESIGHT,** they sometimes charge at trees and termite mounds by mistake. #0025

Hippos whirl their tails around to spray their **poo** over a wide area and mark their territory. #0026

A **GIRAFFE'S** kick is so powerful that it can **KILL A LION.** #0027

10 CREEPY FACTS ABOUT SEA CRITTERS

The **lion's mane jellyfish** can have tentacles **30 metres** long. #0028

A **sea cucumber** can excrete its internal organs to reduce in size! #0029

When a **pistol shrimp** snaps its claw, it makes a noise as loud as a jet engine and heats the water nearby to **4000°C.** #0030

One single **hagfish** can turn a whole bucket of water into **slime** in minutes by releasing horrible mucus from its body. #0031

The **dresser crab** wears **camouflage.** It covers itself with bits of seaweed, sponges and other sea creatures. #0032

All **clownfish** are born **male,** but some later change into **females.** #0033

The **barreleye fish** has a see-through head, with its eyeballs buried deep inside it. It looks through its own head to see! #0034

To eat, **starfish** turn their **stomach inside out** and wrap it around their food. #0035

Handfish walk on the seabed with fins that **work like legs.** #0036

The **deep-sea giant isopod** looks like a **woodlouse,** but is much bigger! #0037

3 SLITHERING SNAKE FACTS

A **spitting cobra** can shoot venom straight into your eyes from **2 metres** away. #0038

Rattlesnakes gain an extra ring for their **rattles** every time they shed their skin. #0039

A **reticulated python** is big enough to swallow a **human** whole!

#0040

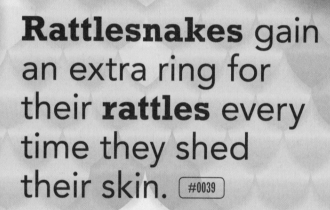

If a predator grabs a **GECKO'S** tail, the tail falls off and **WRIGGLES AND SQUEAKS.** This confuses the predator so the gecko can escape! #0041

5 AWESOME OCTOPUS FACTS

The **MIMIC OCTOPUS** can imitate the shape of a flatfish, a jellyfish, a stingray, a seahorse or a deadly sea snake. #0042

An octopus has **THREE HEARTS** and **NINE BRAINS** – one main brain and a smaller one for each of its tentacles. #0043

Octopuses can change **SHAPE, COLOUR AND TEXTURE,** so they can pretend to be a speckled rock, bumpy coral or frilly seaweed. #0044

The deep-sea **DUMBO OCTOPUS** is like the cartoon elephant because it has massive flappy 'ears' (which are actually fins). #0045

An octopus can distract predators by squirting an **INK CLOUD** that creates an octopus-like shape. #0046

17

4 EVEN MORE BONKERS BIRD FACTS

A **woodpecker** can peck **20 times** in just one second. #0047

Cassowaries can kick so hard with their claws, they can slice through a car door. #0048

Tiny birds called **swiftlets** make nests out of spit. People sometimes collect the nests and use them to make **soup!** #0049

FLAMINGOS eat with their heads **UPSIDE-DOWN.** #0050

A **blue whale** is bigger than **any dinosaur** ever discovered! #0051

A blue whale can hear another blue whale singing from **1,500 kilometres** away. #0052

Whales can't breathe through their **mouths,** only through their **blowholes.** #0053

Bottlenose dolphins can wrap **sea sponges** around their noses to protect them from sharp rocks. #0054

A **humpback whale** can have so many barnacles living on it that they alone weigh as much as six men. #0055

Sperm whales stun their prey by blasting it with an incredibly loud **cracking sound.** #0056

Some Amazon River dolphins are **bright pink!** #0057

Baby whales have hands before they're born. The fingers fuse together to create their fins. #0058

Whales' closest living relatives are **hippos.** #0059

A **Pacific white-sided dolphin** can leap out of the water up to **9 metres** high! #0060

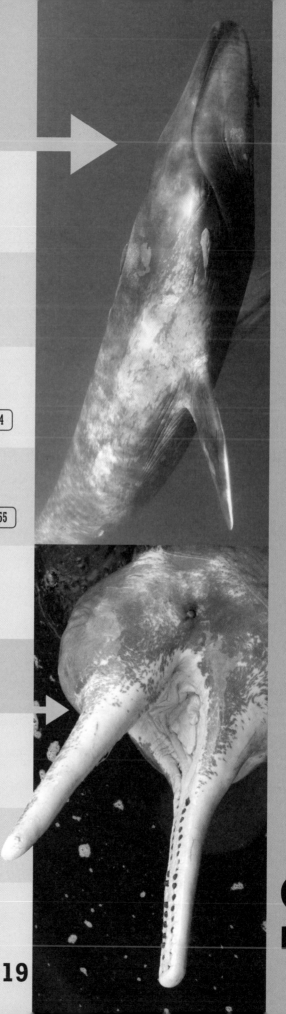

19

10 WHALE AND DOLPHIN WONDERS

44 TOTALLY RANDOM ANIMAL & PLANT FACTS

An ant can carry an object **20 times its own weight**. That's like you carrying a car. #0061

In Africa, colonies of over **20 million safari ants march together** in a huge procession. #0062

The colossal squid has the **biggest eyes** of any animal. **Its eyeballs are the size of footballs.** #0063

Some ants capture ants from other nests to use as **slaves.** #0064

A bristlecone pine tree in California, USA, is thought to be around **4,800 years old** – and it's still growing. #0065

Vampire bats **drink blood** from people and animals. #0066

Robber crabs can **climb trees and crack open coconuts.** #0067

Fungi can grow in soil, around baths – and on your **feet and toenails.** #0068

The bullet ant has the **most painful sting** of any insect. It feels like being shot, and the pain can last for 24 hours. #0069

Rodents' **teeth never stop growing** – they have to gnaw constantly to grind them down. #0070

The giant clam can grow **as big as a sofa.** #0071

Rats **dribble a trail of wee** everywhere they go. #0072

The **super-deadly** death cap toadstool looks very like the **edible** straw mushroom. #0073

Just one mushroom can release **billions of spores** (tiny seeds). #0074

Plant roots are so tough they can **break through concrete.** #0075

Some mushrooms, such as stinkhorns, **smell of rotting meat or even poo.** The smell attracts flies, which spread their spores. #0076

A fungus known as 'winter worm summer grass' **invades a caterpillar's body** in winter (so it looks like a worm) then **grows out of its brain** in summer (so it looks like grass). #0077

Giant Amazon water lily pads are **strong enough for a child to stand on.** #0078

The bee orchid flower looks just like a **real bee.** #0079

The bumblebee bat, the **world's smallest,** is smaller than some bees. #0080

The **giant Bosavi woolly** rat is as **big as a cat.** #0081

Using **echolocation** (bouncing sounds off objects and detecting the echoes), bats can locate an object **as thin as a human hair.** #0082

Cow farts and burps produce around 10% of greenhouse gases. #0083

Bats' wings are made from **skin stretched between their fingers.** #0084

Bracken Cave in Texas, USA, has **20 million bats** living in it. #0085

Each animal has its own **collective noun,** a special name to describe a group of the same species. These nouns include:

a murder of crows, #0086

a leap of leopards, #0087

a prickle of porcupines, #0088

an ugly of walruses, #0089

a mess of iguanas, #0090

a parliament of owls, #0091

a murmuration of starlings, #0092

a knot of toads, #0093

a caravan of camels #0094

and a kindle of kittens. #0095

Tarantula spiders **flick itchy hairs at their enemies.** #0096

Scientists who study bugs (entomologists) have discovered over **5,000 species of dragonflies.** #0097

An electric eel can give you a shock **as bad as one from an electricity socket.** #0098

Centipedes have a **poisonous bite.** A bite from the biggest ones can be dangerous to humans. #0099

Giant African land snails, which grow up to 25 centimetres long, are **a popular food in some countries.** #0100

A flea can jump **more than 100 times its own height** into the air. #0101

Earthworms are both **male and female at the same time.** #0102

Manta rays can **jump up to 3 metres out of the sea** and flap their fins like wings as they 'fly'. #0103

Honeypot ants **hang on the ceiling** of a tunnel in their nests, using their globe-shaped bodies to hold food for others. #0104

10 JAWDROPPING SHARK FACTS

Tiger sharks eat **almost anything.** Some things found inside their stomachs include:

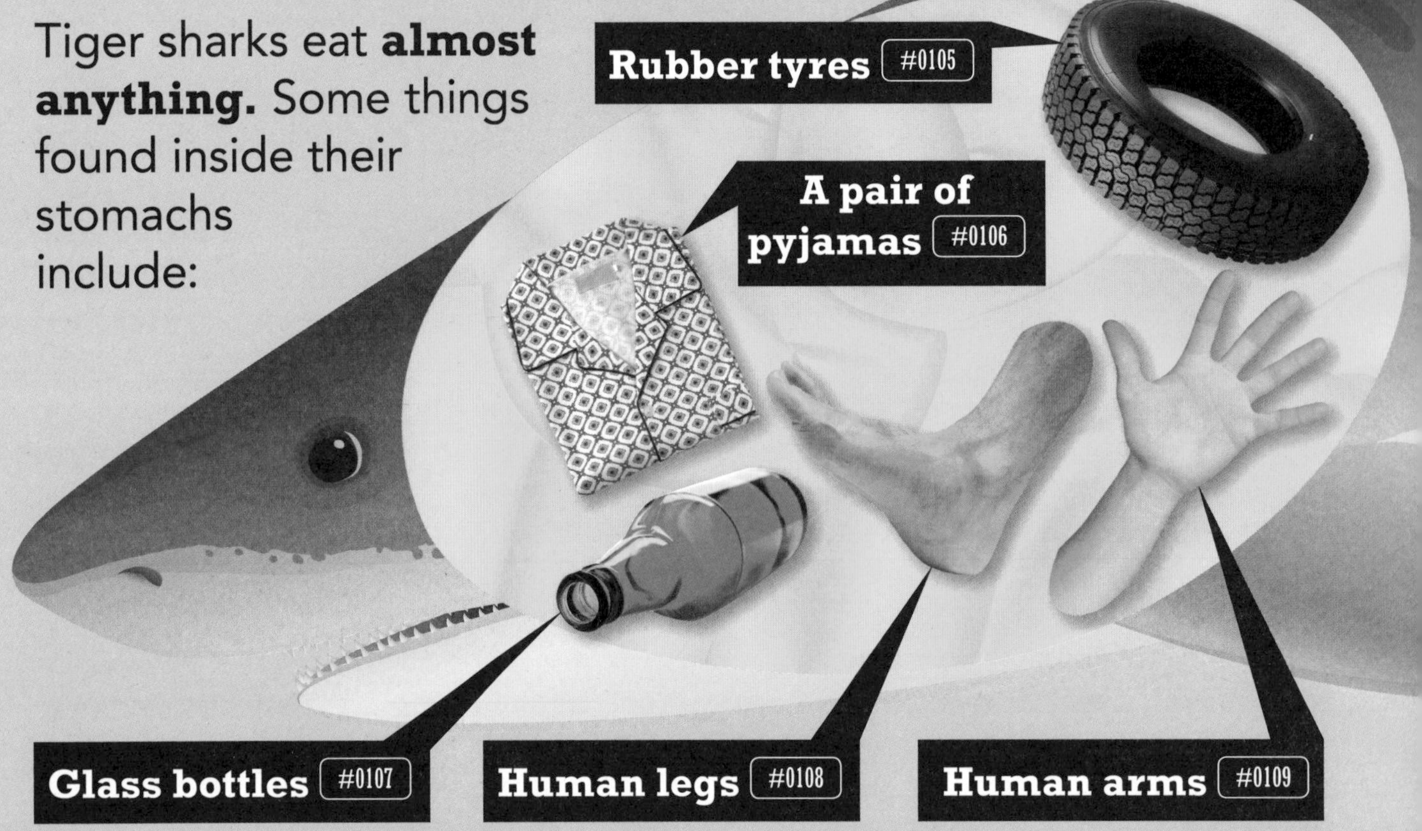

Rubber tyres #0105

A pair of pyjamas #0106

Glass bottles #0107

Human legs #0108

Human arms #0109

Sharks' **skin** isn't scaly, or smooth either – it's covered in **tiny tooth-shaped spikes.** #0110

Sharks have no bones – their skeletons are made of **rubbery cartilage.** #0111

Sharks do **spiral-shaped poos.** #0112

A shark wouldn't really enjoy eating you. They usually **only attack humans by mistake.** #0113

The **CHICKEN** is the most common bird in the world. **SEVEN** There are about chickens for every human on the planet. #0115

10 SUPER-POWERED ANIMAL SENSES

Sharks can sense the **electrical signals** animals' bodies give off when they move. #0116

A male emperor moth can smell a female from **10 kilometres away.** #0117

A **pit viper snake** has heat-sensing 'pits' on its face that allow it to detect its prey's body heat. #0118

A **rat's whiskers** are so sensitive, they can pick up sound vibrations in the air. #0119

Giant pouched rats can be trained to **sniff out** land mines and certain diseases. #0120

When **flies** land on food, they have a quick taste – using the tastebuds on their feet! #0121

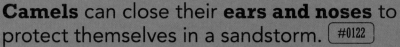

Camels can close their **ears and noses** to protect themselves in a sandstorm. #0122

Some **butterflies** have **ears on their wings,** to listen out for bats that want to eat them. #0123

Octopuses can taste and smell with their **suckers.** #0124

A **chameleon** can point its eyes in **two different directions** at the same time. #0125

Goats and sheep have **rectangular pupils** to help them see sideways. #0126

The **shy-eye shark** covers its eyes with its fins when it sees a bright light. #0127

All **domestic dogs,** however different they are in size, belong to the **same animal species.** #0128

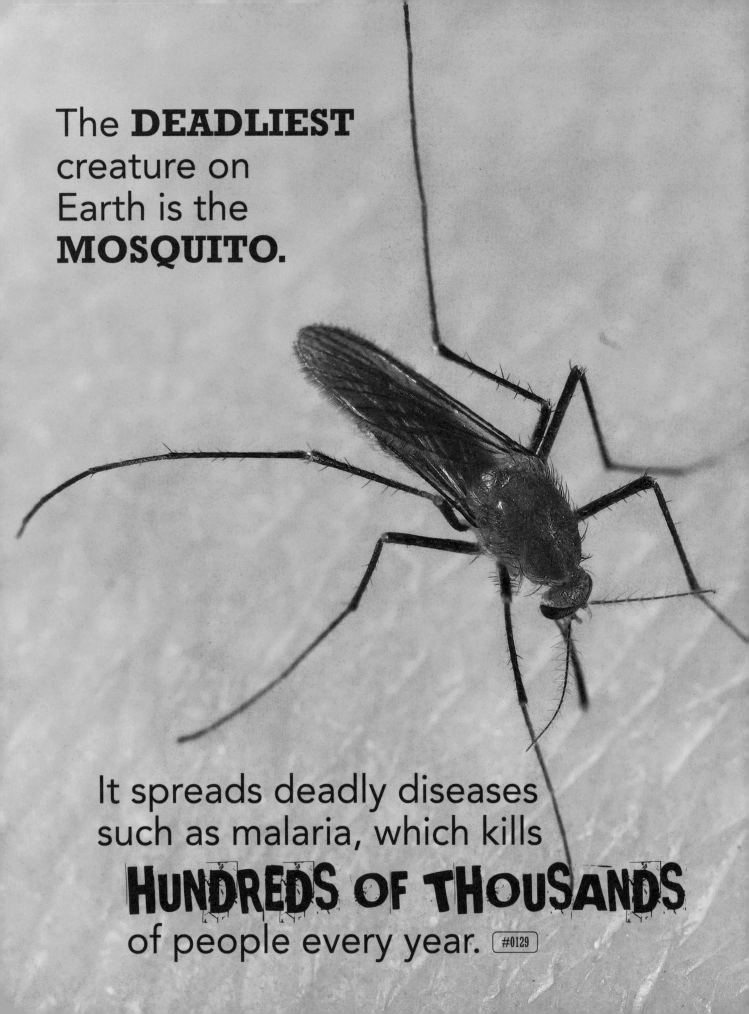

The **DEADLIEST** creature on Earth is the **MOSQUITO.**

It spreads deadly diseases such as malaria, which kills **HUNDREDS OF THOUSANDS** of people every year. #0129

10 BABY ANIMAL BRAINTEASERS

An **ostrich egg** is so **strong** that you could stand on it without breaking it. #0130

Mice breed so fast that in one year, two mice can multiply to become over **4,000 mice.** #0131

A newborn baby **kangaroo** is smaller than your **thumb.** #0132

The greatest number of **yolks** ever found in one chicken **egg** is nine. #0133

Giraffes give birth standing up, so their babies fall **2 metres** onto the ground. Ouch! #0134

A **Surinam toad's** babies hatch out from under the skin on her back. #0135

Sand tiger sharks often start to **eat each other** inside their mum's body before being born. #0136

Baby **tortoise beetles** put predators off by covering themselves in their own poo. #0137

Baby **periodical cicadas** can live for **17 years** underground, yet once they become adults, they live only a **few weeks.** #0138

Baby **elephants** greet each other by **intertwining trunks** and like to play chase games! #0139

3 PECULIAR PREHISTORIC FACTS

In prehistoric times, there were **giant dragonflies** the same size as some modern eagles. #0140

The **closest living relatives** of the dinosaurs are, in fact, **BIRDS!** #0141

Until a living **coelacanth fish** was caught in 1938, scientists thought they had been **extinct** for 65 million years. #0142

10 INCREDIBLE INSECT FACTS

A **quarter** of all animal species are **beetles.** #0143

Antarctic springtail bugs can **reduce their temperature** for the winter. #0144

Bees are found on every continent except Antarctica. #0145

Some **flies** have their eyes located on eyestalks that are longer than their bodies. #0146

Glasswing butterflies have **see-through wings** that look like glass. #0147

'Millipede' means '1,000 legs' – but the millipede with the most legs actually has only **750.** #0148

A large **praying mantis** can catch, kill and eat a **mouse.** #0149

Fireflies can **flash** their glowing tails on and off to send each other **messages.** #0150

In her whole lifetime, a **worker honeybee** makes less than one tenth of a teaspoon of honey. #0151

A **dragonfly** can zoom along at almost **60 kilometres per hour** – faster than a **tiger** can run! #0152

10 SENSATIONAL SPIDER AND SCORPION FACTS

Scorpions **glow in the dark!** If you saw one in the light of the Moon, it would look neon blue. #0153

The **brown recluse spider's** venomous bite eats away at human flesh, leaving a hole that takes weeks to heal. #0154

Most spiders have **eight eyes,** but the **Kauai cave wolf spider** doesn't have **any.** #0155

Spider silk is so strong that a spider silk rope as **thick as a pencil** could stop a **jet aircraft.** #0156

Spiders often recycle their silk by **eating their old web** before spinning a new one. #0157

The **biggest spiderweb ever found** covered a line of trees 180 metres long in Texas, USA. #0158

Baby spiders make parachutes, to float away from their nest, from threads of spider silk. #0159

Scorpions can't sting themselves – they are **immune** to their own **poison.** #0160

A thread of spider silk long enough to reach around the whole world would weigh **less than this book.** #0161

Spiders can spin webs while floating in space. #0162

The **LYREBIRD** can **IMITATE SOUNDS** it hears exactly – including at least **20** other birds' songs, frog calls and even chainsaws, camera shutters and car alarms. #0163

Horseshoe crabs have **bright blue blood!** #0164

CHEETAHS living in desert areas survive without drinking water by eating **MELONS.** #0165

DOGS began living and working with humans more than **30,000 YEARS AGO.** #0166

Wolves have webbed toes. #0167

The **flying fox** isn't a fox – it's a **giant bat,** with wings that can be almost **2 metres** across. #0168

Bar-headed geese fly over the Himalayas at up to **8,000 metres** – almost as high as Mount Everest. #0169

Hummingbirds can beat their wings so fast that they appear **invisible.** #0170

The wandering albatross can have a **3.5-metre wingspan,** so each wing is as long as an adult human. #0171

Flying fish use their fins as wings to glide distances of **180 metres** through the air. #0172

To **fly like a bird,** we would need wings as big as dinner tables! #0173

One type of tiny **midge** can beat its wings more than **1,000 times every second.** #0174

The **longest recorded flight** of a **chicken** is **13 seconds.** It flew just over 100 metres. #0175

A **swarm of flying locusts** can contain **10 billion** insects and be so thick it blocks out the sunlight. #0176

In 1973, a **Ruppell's vulture** flew into an aircraft at an altitude of **11,000 metres** – the highest bird flight ever recorded. #0177

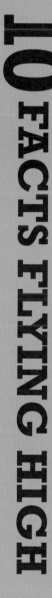

5 LUDICROUS LIZARD FACTS

KOMODO DRAGONS sometimes dig up human graves looking for a snack. #0178

When threatened, **HORNED LIZARDS** squirt **BLOOD** from their **EYES** to confuse predators. #0179

Geckos can cling onto ceilings using thousands of tiny hairs on their **FEET**. #0180

A **CHAMELEON** can flick out its tongue to **15 CENTIMETRES** long in one thirtieth of a second. #0181

BASILISK LIZARDS can run on water. #0182

A fully grown tree produces **ENOUGH OXYGEN** in one year to keep a **FAMILY OF FOUR** breathing.

#0183

10 SUPER-SMART FACTS ABOUT ANIMALS

An **African grey parrot** named Alex learned to count, sort out **shapes** and say 150 different words. #0184

Kanzi the **bonobo,** a type of chimpanzee, can understand around **3,000 English words.** #0185

A clever crow named Betty worked out how to make a **wire hook** to fish food out of a jar. #0186

Chimps poke sticks into termite nests, wait until termites crawl onto them and then lick them clean. #0187

Some **Japanese macaques** wash potatoes in seawater to clean them and add salty seasoning. #0188

Ants can use their antennae to tell other ants how to **solve a maze.** #0189

Bonobos use plants and minerals as **medicines** to treat worms, diarrhoea and stomach ache. #0190

Killer whales have been found to enjoy looking at **books!** #0191

An **octopus** can open a **screw-top jar** with its tentacles. #0192

An **elephant** can recognize itself in a **mirror.** #0193

Sociable **weaver birds** use grass to build huge nests with space for **200 or more birds.** #0194

How many times have you moved house? **ORANGUTANS** build themselves a new **NEST** of leaves and branches **EVERY NIGHT!** #0195

When **BEAVERS** build a **DAM,** they can completely change the **DIRECTION OF A RIVER.** #0196

A **giant squid's oesophagus** (the tube that food passes through to get to the stomach) runs right through its **brain.** #0197

Termite nests can tower up to **9 METRES TALL.**

That's about

eight times

the size of an average eight-year-old. #0198

10 FACTS ABOUT HUNGRY HUNTERS

Velvet worms shoot streams of **sticky glue** on their prey to trap them. #0199

The **tarantula hawk wasp** stings a tarantula to paralyse it, then lays its egg on it. When the wasp baby hatches, it eats the tarantula alive! #0200

The **death adder** wiggles the tip of its tail to look like a **tasty worm,** then when birds and lizards come to eat it, the adder eats them! #0201

Wild cats called **margays** can make a noise like a baby monkey. When the mother comes to look for her baby, the margay attacks! #0202

Killer whales sometimes **surf right out of the sea** and up onto the beach to grab their seal dinner! #0203

The **green heron** drops insects or bits of bread onto the water to lure **tasty fish** to the surface. #0204

Tigers in the Sundarbans area of India enjoy **snacking on humans!** They catch fishermen by sneaking up on them from behind. #0205

Net-casting spiders throw a special **net made of silk** over passing insects to trap them. #0206

The **stonefish** disguises itself as a stone, then grabs passing prey in its mouth in less than one tenth of a second. #0207

The **goliath tigerfish** of the Congo River is so fierce, it even attacks crocodiles! #0208

5 FACTS ABOUT INCREDIBLE JOURNEYS

ARCTIC TERNS migrate from the Arctic to the Antarctic and back every year, flying **70,000 KILOMETRES.** #0209

SALMON are born in streams, then swim all the way to the ocean. Before they die, they swim back to the **EXACT SAME STREAM** they came from to lay their eggs. #0210

MONARCH BUTTERFLIES can find their way to the very same spot where their great-great-grandparents hatched out. #0211

COCONUTS have been known to float **10,000 KILOMETRES** across an ocean before growing into a tree on another continent. #0212

Every spring, millions of **RED CRABS** on Christmas Island in the Indian Ocean migrate from forests to the **SEA** to breed. A few weeks later, their babies migrate back again! #0213

PLATYPUSES and **ECHIDNAS,** furry and spiny burrowing creatures found in Australia and New Guinea, are the only **MAMMALS** that lay **EGGS.** #0214

Three-toed sloths have **moths** living in their fur. #0215

Sea-slugs are **hermaphrodites** – they have both male and female reproductive organs. This increases their chances of finding a mate! #0216

4 BLINK-AND-YOU'LL-MISS-THEM CAMOUFLAGE FACTS

Leaf insects look like **LEAVES.** They have holes and brown patches to make their camouflage more realistic. #0217

The **OWL BUTTERFLY** has bright eye spots that make it look like an **OWL'S FACE.** #0218

The **swallowtail butterfly caterpillar** avoids being eaten by resembling a **bird dropping.** #0219

Stick insects trick predators because they look like **walking twigs** and often their eggs look like seeds. #0220

5 FACTS ABOUT MONKEYING AROUND

GORILLAS make burping and grumbling noises when they are **HAPPY.** #0221

Gorillas sometimes eat their own **POO!** #0222

The **PROBOSCIS MONKEY** has a huge droopy nose, the biggest of any primate. #0223

Monkeys always peel **BANANAS** before they eat them – from the bottom end, not the stalk end. #0224

JAPANESE MACAQUES use natural hot springs to enjoy a **WARM BATH.** #0225

The heaviest insect, the **GIANT WETA,** weighs up to

70 grams.

That's as much as a satsuma. #0226

10 PLANT-TASTIC FACTS

When **maple trees** are attacked by insects, they release chemicals into the air, to warn other trees. #0227

A **squirting cucumber** explodes to shoot seeds and slime up to **6 metres** through the air. #0228

One **baobab tree** in South Africa has such a huge, thick trunk that a drinks bar has been built inside it. #0229

A single **banyan tree** can have **hundreds** of trunks. #0230

Pebble plants in the desert hide from hungry animals by looking exactly like stones. #0231

The castor bean plant makes a **poison** so deadly, one teaspoon of it could kill **hundreds of people.** #0232

The meat-eating giant pitcher plant **from the Philippines** has traps so large it can swallow a **rat.** #0233

A **bamboo stalk** can grow more than **1 metre** in a single day. #0234

Giant redwoods are the world's tallest trees, reaching **115 metres** high, with trunks 5 metres across. #0235

The massive **titan arum flower** of Indonesia can reach **3 metres tall** – and smells like rotting meat! #0236

45

A **fish tapeworm** can grow inside a human's intestines! #0237

The **cordyceps fungus** compels an ant to climb to the top of a grass stalk, before growing out of its head and releasing its spores. #0238

Boxer crabs carry around stinging **sea anemones** to sting their enemies! #0239

A **tongue-eating louse** eats a fish's **tongue,** then takes its place and lives within the fish's mouth! #0240

As a **tick** sucks blood from its host, it grows up to **10 times** its original body size. #0241

The biggest **bloodsucking leeches** are as long as your arm and as wide as a banana. #0242

Honey guide birds lead **honey badgers** to bees' nests. The badger breaks open the nest and the bird gets a share! #0243

The **cuckoo** lays its egg in another bird's nest, then that bird raises the cuckoo chick! #0244

A **leech** can suck up to **10 times** its weight in blood. #0245

Sharks let **pilot fish** swim inside their mouths to clean their teeth! #0246

TIGERS love SWIMMING!

However, they hate getting water in their eyes, so to keep their head dry they will often get in the water backwards. #0247

Chapter 2

BIZARRE
HUMAN
BODY BITS

The loudest **SCREAM** on record was **129** decibels.

That's as loud as a

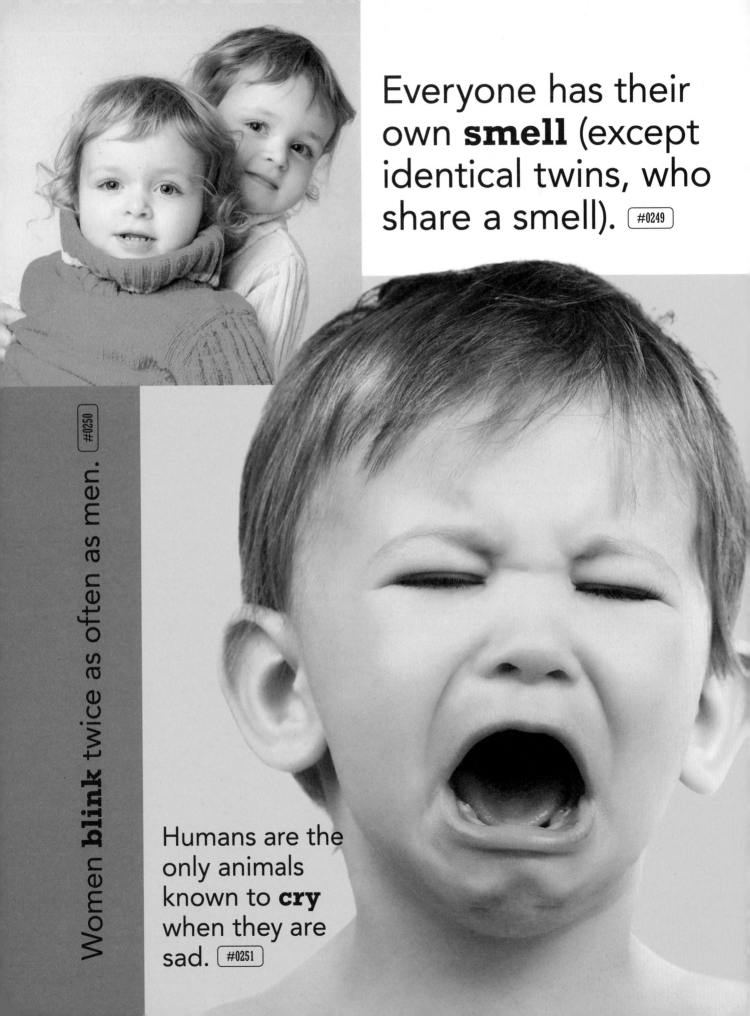

Everyone has their own **smell** (except identical twins, who share a smell). #0249

Women **blink** twice as often as men. #0250

Humans are the only animals known to **cry** when they are sad. #0251

The muscle that exerts the most pressure for its size is the masseter, or **JAW** muscle. #0252

You have to use about **300 MUSCLES** just to stand up without falling over. #0253

Astronauts' muscles get **WEAKER** the longer they spend in space. This is because their muscles don't have to work to resist gravity. #0254

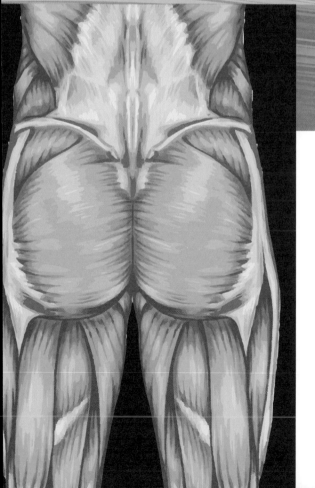

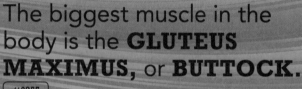

The biggest muscle in the body is the **GLUTEUS MAXIMUS,** or **BUTTOCK.** #0255

DIMPLES are caused by muscles pulling on the skin of your face. #0256

51

10 THOUGHT-PROVOKING BRAIN FACTS

The human brain can do about **100 trillion** (100,000,000,000,000) calculations per second. #0257

If you spread the wrinkly covering of your brain out flat, it would be as **big as a newspaper.** #0258

If someone cut into your brain with a **knife,** you wouldn't feel any **pain.** #0259

There is evidence that a person can remain conscious for a few seconds after having their **head chopped off.** #0260

A normal human brain can store more information than a **room full of books.** #0261

If **half** of your brain was removed... you could live quite normally! #0262

A newborn baby already has all its brain cells. #0264

The brain can shrink up to **15%** as it ages. #0263

US scientist Chet Fleming has invented a device for keeping **a severed human head alive.** (It hasn't been built yet!) #0265

The brain works harder when you're **asleep** than when you're awake. #0266

Lee Redmond of Utah, USA, grew her **FINGERNAILS** to almost a

metre LONG.

(Unfortunately, they were then broken off in a car accident!) #0267

53

35 RANDOM
BODY FACTS

If all the **blood vessels** in your body were laid out in a line they would reach **twice around the world.** #0268

Human bone is **stronger than concrete or steel.** #0269

You have over **200 bones** in your body. #0270

Over half of all the bones in your body are in your **feet and hands.** #0271

People used to **drill holes in skulls** to cure headaches. #0272

The ancient Aztecs used **human thighbones to make musical instruments.** #0273

The body rots away after death, but **bones can last for thousands of years.** #0274

After the age of about 30, people's **skeletons start to shrink.** #0275

The **smallest bone** in your body is in your **ears** and is 0.3 cm long. #0276

Bones can repair themselves if they get broken, but teeth can't. #0277

Your **funny bone isn't a bone**, but a sensitive nerve running past your elbow joint. #0278

Some snores are as loud as a road drill. #0279

You spend around **a third of your life** asleep. #0280

When you dream, you don't **invent people's faces** – they are people you've seen before. #0281

The record for a human lasting without sleep is **18 days, 21 hours and 40 minutes.** #0282

An Italian man named Francesco Lentini had **three legs.** #0283

People can have **artificial** legs, arms, feet, noses, hearts, hips, teeth, ears and hands. #0284

Weird things have been found **inside people's stomachs,** including...

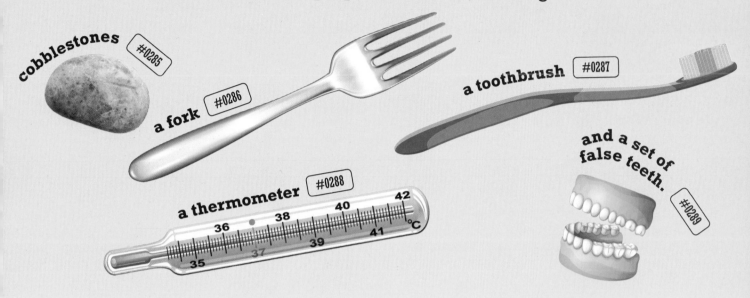

cobblestones #0285

a fork #0286

a toothbrush #0287

a thermometer #0288

and a set of false teeth. #0289

You are **taller in the morning** because gravity squashes your body slightly during the day. #0290

Your fingers have **no muscles.** They are **controlled by muscles in your arms.** #0291

Some people have **five fingers and one thumb** on each hand. #0292

If you **stretch your arms wide,** the distance between your fingertips **is the same as your height.** #0293

Doctors have mistakenly **left things inside people's bodies** after surgery, including a **needle** #0294, **scissors** #0295, **tweezers** #0296, **pliers** #0297 and **a sponge.** #0298

The human body contains around **75 trillion cells.** #0299

A typical human cell is **10 microns across** – about the size of a single speck of talcum powder. #0300

The **longest cells** in the human body are **nerve cells** reaching from the toes to the spine. #0301

In the time it takes to read this sentence, **30 million** of your cells have **died and been replaced.** #0302

In 1848, a railway worker named Phineas Gage survived having an **iron bar blown though his brain** by an explosion. He lived until 1860. #0303

People with **synaesthesia** get their senses mixed up – they may see sounds, feel colours, or taste musical notes. #0304

A man grows about **five metres** of **beard** hair in a lifetime. #0305

10 HIGHLY SENSITIVE SENSES FACTS

When you touch something, a message zooms from your fingers to your brain at **150 kilometres an hour** – as fast as a **speeding train.** #0306

Some people can **pop their eyeballs** right out of their head. #0307

You can't **taste** things if your tongue is **dry.** #0308

People who've lost an arm or a leg sometimes feel pain as if it's still there. It's called a **'phantom limb'.** #0309

Children's **hearing** is better than adults'. #0310

Some blind people can sense where objects are by using **echolocation,** as bats do. #0311

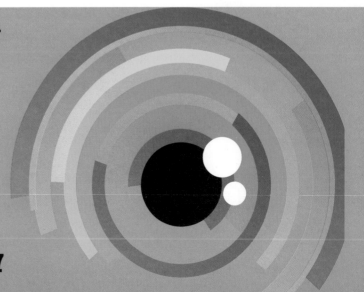

Your nose can remember **50,000** different scents. #0312

Human eyes can detect over **a million** different **colours** and **shades.** #0313

All your life, your **nose** and **ears** very slowly keep getting **bigger...** #0314

... but your **eyeballs** stay almost the same size for your whole life. #0315

10 BARMY BLOOD AND BREATHING FACTS

Your **heart** will beat between **2 and 3 billion** times over the course of a lifetime. #0316

If you spread all the breathing surfaces inside your lungs out flat, they would be the size of a **tennis court.** #0317

With every breath, you take in **air molecules** breathed out by **dinosaurs.** #0318

On deep dives without breathing equipment, a diver's lungs shrink to the size of **grapefruits.** #0319

Some people who've had a **heart transplant** say they start liking the same food, hobbies and colours as their heart donor. #0320

The **heart muscles** squeeze so hard they could squirt blood **10 metres** through the air. #0321

Blood is as salty as **seawater.** #0322

It takes about **45 seconds** for a blood cell to zoom around the body. #0323

Blood cells are made inside your **bones.** #0324

Octopuses have **blue blood** and insects have **yellow blood.** #0325

You make enough **SALIVA** each day to fill five teacups. #0326

Urine is mostly water, so it can be **drunk for survival** in an emergency. #0327

If the body's **temperature** **drops below** 21°C, it's usually fatal.

4 LITTLE FACTS ABOUT LITTLE PEOPLE

More babies are born on a **TUESDAY** than on any other day. #0329

Babies start **dreaming** before birth. #0330

Babies are born with around **300 bones,** but by adulthood only 206 are left. #0331

Babies are born able to **swim** and to hold their breath underwater. #0332

5 BODY INGREDIENTS

An average human body contains enough:

COPPER
to make
1 centimetre
of thin copper
wire #0333

CARBON
to make
15,000 pencils #0334

ALUMINIUM
to make
a piece of foil the size
of your palm #0335

IRON
to make
a large nail #0336

ARSENIC
to kill a rat #0337

10 FACTS ABOUT WHAT GOES IN... AND WHAT COMES OUT

A human consumes as much food and drink in a lifetime as the weight of **one medium-sized blue whale.** #0338

If your **intestines** were stretched out, they would be more than four times as long as your body. #0339

You can eat upside down, as **special muscles** squeeze food towards your stomach. #0340

Eating snot can be good for you – it teaches your body to fight off germs. #0341

If you lose part of your **liver,** it can regrow itself. #0342

You can live without a **stomach.** #0343

Stomach acid is strong enough to dissolve metal. #0344

The average person **farts 14 times** a day. #0345

You have **billions of bacteria** living in your intestines. They help you digest food. #0346

Your stomach avoids **eating itself** by coating its own inside with thick mucus! #0347

Your brain is made up of **85% WATER** – the same as a **CABBAGE!** #0348

If you wear **headphones,** your ears make extra **earwax.** #0349

Most people sweat about **two teacups of liquid** per day, but it can be as much as a small bucketful! #0351

Your saliva (spit), tears, earwax, snot and sweat all contain **chemicals that kill germs.** #0350

You can have a heart, lung, kidney, liver, hand or even face **TRANSPLANTED** from another person. #0352

Sometimes if a patient is given a **FAKE MEDICINE,** it can affect them like a real drug because they believe they will get better – it's called the 'placebo effect'. #0353

Before anaesthetics, people having a limb amputated would **bite down on a piece of leather** to help deal with the pain. #0354

Cola drinks and **tomato ketchup** were once sold as **medicines.** #0355

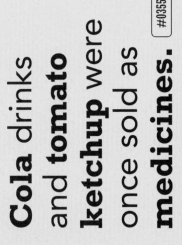

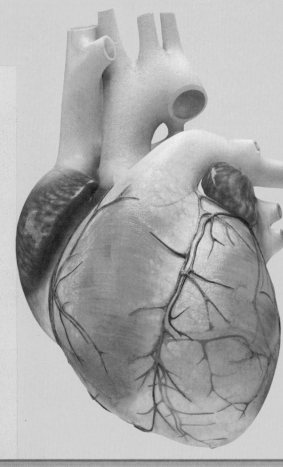

medicine

10 FACTS ABOUT YOUR OUTSIDES

Every day, you shed about **40 million** dead skin cells. #0356

Dust is mainly dead skin cells. #0357

You have about **5 million hairs** on your body. #0358

Your skin is as heavy as wearing **four winter coats.** #0359

In a lifetime, you'll leave up to **20 kilograms** of dead skin lying around. #0360

Fingernails and **toenails** grow faster in hot weather. #0361

Most people have tiny creepy-crawlies called **mites** living around their eyelashes. #0362

Your **nose gets runny** when you cry because tears from the eyes drain into the nose. #0363

Xie Qiuping of China holds the record for the longest hair in the world, at **5.6 metres.** #0364

Humans have been decorating their nails for more than **5,000 years.** #0365

10 AMAZING BODY NUMBERS

If all the **DNA** in your body was unravelled and stretched out, it could reach to the **Sun and back.** #0366

Frenchwoman Jeanne Calment lived to be **122 years old,** longer than anyone else on record. #0367

A Russian woman, Mrs Vassilyev, is thought to have had **69 children** – 32 twins, 21 triplets and 16 quadruplets. #0368

Every human started off as **one cell,** for about the first half an hour that they existed. #0369

A sneeze zooms out of your nose and mouth at around **150 kilometres** an hour. #0370

Robert Wadlow, the **tallest person ever,** measured **2.72 metres** and had **size 36 feet.** #0371

Lucia Zarate, the **smallest person ever**, was **51 centimetres** tall and weighed 2.1 kilograms. #0372

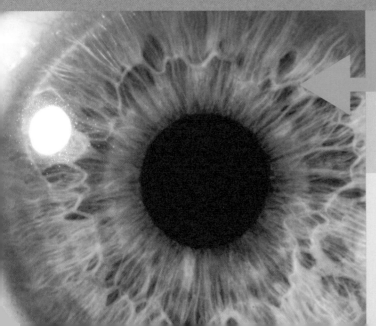

The **human eye** can see stars that are **millions of miles away.** #0373

Park Ranger **Roy Sullivan** survived being struck by lightning **seven times.** #0374

Charles Osborne of Iowa, USA, **hiccupped** non-stop for 68 years. #0375

Because you blink around

**15 TIMES
A MINUTE...**

... you actually spend two years of your waking life with your **EYES SHUT.** #0376

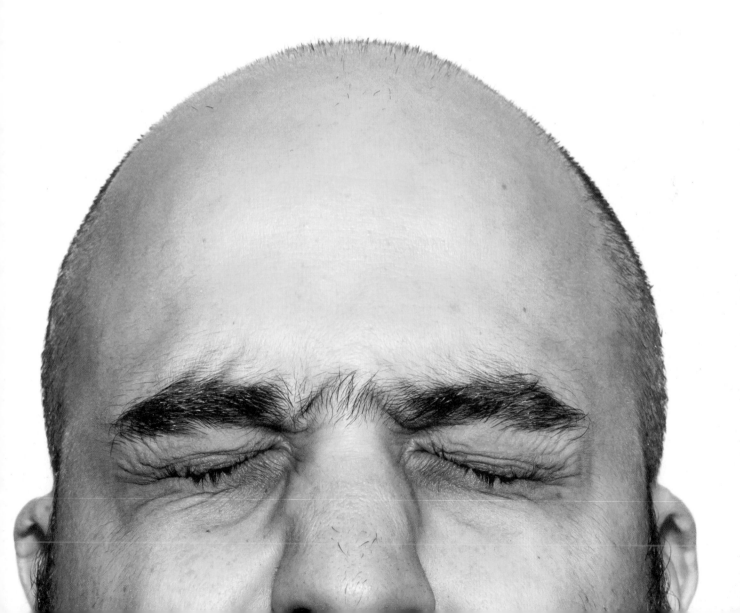

THE GREAT WALL OF CHINA was started around 500 BC and is over **21,000 KILOMETRES LONG.** That's as far as the distance from the North Pole to the South Pole! #0377

Chapter 3

HISTORY
YOU
HAVE TO
HEAR

4 FACTS ON CHINA'S SECRET ARMY

Emperor **Qin Shi Huangdi** of China (259 BC–210 BC) wanted to **live forever,** so he built a huge burial mound to protect his body in the afterlife. #0378

At least **8,000 CLAY SOLDIERS** guard the tomb, as well as **130 CHARIOTS** and **670 HORSES.** #0379

The burial mound is believed to contain **booby traps to protect his body,** which is also surrounded by rivers of poisonous **mercury!** #0380

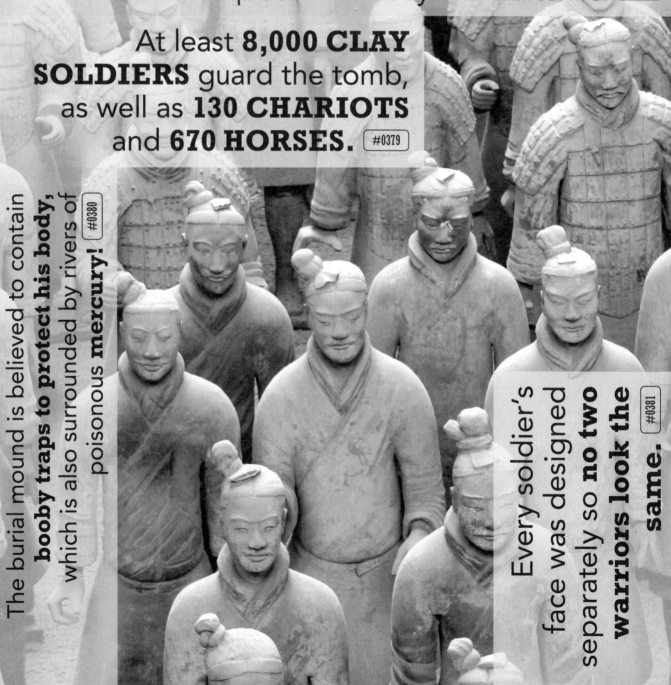

Every soldier's face was designed separately so **no two warriors look the same.** #0381

10 FACTS ABOUT THE WORLD'S BLOODIEST BATTLES

The world's **longest war** lasted for **116 years**. It was between England and France and started in 1337. #0382

The world's **shortest war** lasted just **38 minutes**, when a British fleet attacked the island of Zanzibar in 1896. #0383

Between **62 and 78 million** people died during World War II (1939–1945). #0384

During the Mongol conquests (1207–1472) **17% of the world's population died.** #0385

Nearly **2 million** German and Russian soldiers were **killed or wounded** during a battle at Stalingrad (1942–1943). #0386

During the Battle of the Somme, on 1 July 1916, around **19,240 of the British army were killed.** #0387

Around **51,000** soldiers died in a **three-day battle** during the American Civil War (1861–1865). #0388

Confederate General 'Stonewall' Jackson was mistakenly **killed by his own men.** #0389

The **largest naval battle** took place at Salamis in Greece about **2,500 years** ago. #0390

The **largest tank and aerial battles** happened at the same time, at Kursk in 1942, between Germans and Russians. #0391

5 EXPLORATORY FACTS ABOUT EXPLORERS

The Norwegian explorer **ROALD AMUNDSEN** was the first man to reach the **SOUTH POLE,** in 1911. #0392

During his lifetime, explorer **IBN BATTUTA** (1304–1368 or 1369) travelled 120,000 kilometres by foot, camel and ship – as far as three times around the world. #0393

On an expedition in 1862, British explorer **JOHN SPEKE** became temporarily deaf after a **BEETLE** crawled into his ear and he tried to remove it with a knife! #0394

In 1860, **ROBERT BURKE** and **WILLIAM WILLS** walked across Australia in search of an **INLAND SEA.** They discovered there was no sea, but then died trying to get home. #0395

In 1642, Dutch explorer **ABEL TASMAN** sailed round the whole of **AUSTRALIA** without ever realizing it existed! #0396

Instead of using maps, **AUSTRALIAN ABORIGINALS** sang songs about landmarks such as rocks, trees and waterholes to help them remember paths across the continent.

#0397

4 FACTS ABOUT LOOOONG MARCHES

In 1846, the American **Mormon Battalion** marched over **3,000 kilometres** from Council Bluffs, Iowa, to San Diego, California. Their march helped the US government to gain control of large areas of the American continent. #0398

From 1096, Christian soldiers marched and sailed out of **EUROPE** to the Holy Land in an attempt to rid it of Muslim control. Many thousands of people, including children, took part. #0399

In 334 BC, **ALEXANDER THE GREAT** led his army of around **50,000 MACEDONS** out of Europe into Asia on a journey that lasted until he died 11 years later. #0400

In 1812, Emperor **Napoleon** of France led his Grand Army of **685,000** men on a mission to invade Russia. It's estimated that there were only **70,000 survivors**. #0401

5 EMPIRE FACTS THAT TOTALLY RULE

The **LARGEST-EVER EMPIRE** in the world was the **BRITISH EMPIRE,** which peaked in 1922 when it covered over a fifth of the world's lands. #0402

The **ROMAN EMPIRE** included millions of people living over a large area and they kept track of everyone by counting them! Just like our modern-day **CENSUS.** #0403

The empire that lasted the longest was the ancient empire of **CHINA** – for well over **2,000 YEARS!** #0404

Today, **JAPAN** is the only country in the world that calls itself an **EMPIRE** and has an emperor. #0405

At one time, European colonial empires and Chinese and Japanese empires controlled **EVERY MODERN-DAY COUNTRY IN THE WORLD** except Iran, Thailand, Afghanistan, Bhutan and Liberia, which were never fully conquered. #0406

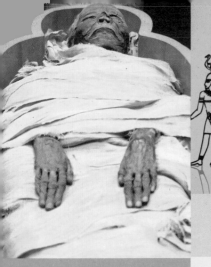

10 MYSTICAL FACTS ABOUT ANCIENT EGYPT

The **Great Pyramid** in Egypt was built in **2560 BC** and was originally 146.5 metres tall! #0407

The pyramid is made up of **2.3 million limestone blocks...** #0408

... and took 100,000 workers **20 years** to complete! #0409

The Egyptian **god of the dead** was called Anubis. He had the head of a jackal. #0410

The Egyptian **goddess of pregnancy and childbirth** was a hippopotamus called Taweret. #0411

Queen Hatshepsut of Egypt took the title of king. She dressed as a king and even wore a false beard! #0412

Tutankhamun was only nine years old when he became pharaoh. #0413

Children in Ancient Egypt didn't wear much clothing, because it was so hot. #0414

When an Egyptian body was **mummified,** its brain was removed through one of its nostrils... #0415

... and the liver, intestines, lungs and stomach were put in **canopic jars.** #0416

The **ANCIENT POLYNESIAN PEOPLES** had no navigation instruments, but sailed across big distances of open sea using only **THEIR SENSES!**

They would watch the stars, feel the motion of the waves, listen to wildlife and follow weather signs. #0417

5 FACTS ABOUT VOTES FOR WOMEN

In 1718, a small group of female Swedish craftworkers were the **first women in the world** allowed to vote in elections. #0418

In 1756, Lydia Chapin Taft became the **first woman voter in North America** when she voted in Massachusetts Colony, then ruled by Britain. #0419

The first country to give all women the vote was **New Zealand, in 1893.** #0420

British women aged 30 and over got the vote in **1918,** while women in **Switzerland** had to wait until **1971.** #0421

Women in **Saudi Arabia** were first given voting rights in 2015. #0422

3 ARTY FACTS

The world's **oldest painting** is over **40,000 years old** – a red sphere of paint and handprints on a cave wall in El Castillo in Spain. #0423

One of the most **expensive paintings** in the world is 'The Card Players' by Paul Cezanne, which sold in 2011 for **£160 million.** #0424

The oldest pieces of **pottery** in the world were found in 2012 by Chinese archaeologists. At **20,000 years old,** they were made at a time when much of the world was covered with ice! #0425

3 FACTS ABOUT WONDROUS WALLS

During the AD 770s, King **Offa of Mercia** in central England ordered a border to be dug to keep the Welsh out of his kingdom. The ditch is **20 metres wide** and can still be seen today. #0428

The **ancient wall** that stretches round Rome is **19 kilometres long, 16 metres tall** and has **383 towers, 18 main gates – and 116 toilets!** #0427

Hadrian's Wall, a **120-kilometre wall,** was built for the Roman Emperor Hadrian to prevent attacks by raiders from the north of Britain. #0426

10 FACTS ABOUT GODS AND EMPERORS

The Japanese believe that their emperor is a descendant of **Amaterasu,** the goddess of the Sun and the Universe. #0429

The current Japanese emperor, Akihito, is the **125th emperor of Japan.** #0430

The Chinese emperor was called the **'Son of Heaven'.** #0431

In 331 BC, **Alexander the Great** decided that the Egyptian sky-god, Amun, was his real father! #0432

Napoleon Bonaparte became Emperor of France in 1804 – yet he was not even born in France! #0433

Napoleon made his **three brothers kings** and his **sister a grand duchess.** #0434

The Roman emperor, **Caligula,** went mad and appointed his horse, Incitatus, a priest. #0435

Diocletian was the first Roman emperor ever to resign. He retired to a palace in Croatia and grew cabbages instead. #0436

After he died in 44 BC, **Julius Caesar** was officially recognized as a **god** by the Roman State. #0437

When **Ogedei Khan** of the Mongol empire died in AD 1241, the Mongol armies fighting in Western Europe had to go home to Asia to elect a new emperor. #0438

4 GOLDEN NUGGETS ABOUT ANCIENT GREECE

In the Greek state of **Sparta, boys** were taken from their mothers at seven years old and sent to boot camps, where they were brought up in packs and competed in mock fights. #0439

The Ancient Greeks invented the **THEATRE,** building huge amphitheatres for plays. All the actors were men – even those playing women's parts! #0440

The Ancient Greeks worshipped **many gods,** including twelve main gods and goddesses who lived on Mount Olympus. #0441

At 20, the Spartans were given a **TOUGH FITNESS AND LEADERSHIP TEST** in order to join the military, and their duty didn't end until they were 60. #0442

82

5 FASCINATING VIKING FACTS

The name **'VIKING'** comes from a language called Old Norse and means **'A PIRATE RAID'**. #0443

Viking **LONGBOATS** were cleverly designed to **FLOAT HIGH** in the water and **LAND ON BEACHES** – so the Vikings could jump out of the ship and join a raid quickly. #0444

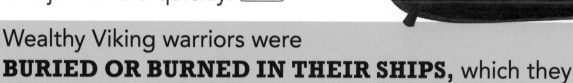

Wealthy Viking warriors were **BURIED OR BURNED IN THEIR SHIPS,** which they believed would carry them into the next world. #0445

The word **'BERSERK'** comes from 'Berserkers' – terrifying Viking warriors who wore wolf or bear skin and howled in battle like wild animals. #0446

Vikings believed in several gods, including **THOR,** the god of thunder. Our word **'THURSDAY'** is named after Thor ('Thor's Day'). #0447

A Roman **centurion** was in command of 80 men, divided up into ten units of eight men each. #0448

The Romans discovered **concrete!** They mixed lime, volcanic ash and water. #0449

Boys were **beaten** in Roman schools if they made mistakes! #0450

In Ancient Rome, urine was collected, and used for **tanning leather** and **cleaning togas.** #0451

The **Pantheon**, a temple to the gods, was built in AD 126. It is still the world's largest unreinforced concrete dome. #0452

Roman legions were named after their **qualities** or the **places** they served in. #0453

The Romans made **hamburgers** more than 2,000 years ago and ate **take-away food** from local bars. #0454

The world's **first fire engine** was invented by the engineer Hero, from Roman Egypt. #0455

The Romans heated their houses with the world's **first central heating system,** known as a hypocaust. #0456

While everyone else used scythes to cut corn, the Romans developed an early **combine harvester!** #0457

The Ancient Romans used guard dogs to guard their homes and, just like today, they even had **'BEWARE OF THE DOG'** signs. #0458

Some of the stones in the ancient circle of stones at **STONEHENGE** in southern England (constructed between 3100 and 1600 BC) weigh around **26** tons.

They are over **5** metres tall. #0459

10 FACTS ON FIERCE FEMALE RULERS

In 1762, **Empress Catherine the Great** of Russia took the throne from her husband! #0460

The first woman to become a prime minister was **Sirimavo Bandaranaike,** who governed Sri Lanka from 1960–65, 1970–77 and 1994–2000. #0461

Queen Victoria of England ruled from 1837 for 63 years and 216 days! #0462

Many of Queen Victoria's **40 grandchildren** became kings and queens of other European countries. #0463

Margaret Thatcher was **Britain's first female prime minister** and was nicknamed **'The Iron Lady'** because of her strong-willed leadership style. #0464

None of the 43 American presidents and numerous vice-presidents have been women. #0465

The first woman to become a president was **Isabel Peron,** who governed Argentina in 1974. #0466

In 2012, **Queen Elizabeth II** celebrated 60 years on the British throne. #0467

Until 2013, women had ruled the Netherlands for **over 100 years!** #0468

Mary Queen of Scots was only six days old when she became Queen of Scotland in 1542. #0469

3 FACTS ABOUT THE INSPIRATIONAL INCAS

The Incas of South America could not read or write, so they used lengths of knotted, coloured strings called **quipus** to keep records. #0470

The Incas built around **40,000 kilometres** of **roads.** Messengers ran along them day and night carrying messages for the emperor. #0471

The Incas cut and fitted together **stone bricks** so perfectly that their walls didn't need any mortar to hold them in place. #0472

10 FACTS ABOUT RUTHLESS RULERS

In 1258, the Mongol army attacked Baghdad and killed at least **200,000 of its 1 million people.** #0473

When an Iranian city rebelled against his high taxes in the 1400s, Central Asian conqueror Timur **killed all 70,000 inhabitants.** #0474

The Aztecs of Central America **sacrificed humans to satisfy their gods!** #0475

In the 1500s, Russian ruler Ivan the Terrible **killed his own son** during an argument. #0476

Kaiser Wilhelm II of Germany abdicated in 1918 after almost **10 million soldiers** died during World War I between 1914 and 1918. #0477

During **Pol Pot's** rule of Cambodia, between 1975 and 1979, about **2 million** people were killed – a third of the population. #0478

In the 540s BC, **King Nabonidus of Babylon** ate **grass** and thought he was a **goat!** #0479

When feared dictator **Joseph Stalin** had a stroke in 1953, his ministers and police were too scared to call a doctor for him! #0480

Idi Amin, president of Uganda from 1971 to 1979, killed up to 500,000 opponents. #0481

In 1976, **President Jean-Bédel Bokassa,** military ruler of the Central African Republic, declared himself **emperor!** #0482

3 FACTS ABOUT SAILING THE SEVEN SEAS

Between 1676 and 1710, **William Dampier** from England completed **three round-the-world voyages** – one time as a pirate, raiding enemy ships! #0483

In 1895, **Joshua Slocum** set out to become the first man to **sail around the world by himself,** though he did stop many times along the route. #0484

The first man to sail alone around the world without stopping was **Englishman Robin Knox-Johnston,** who did it in 313 days in 1968–69. The current record is 45 days and 13 hours. #0485

4 ANCIENT FACTS ABOUT CIVILIZATIONS

Writing **words** using pictures and signs first appeared about **5,500 years ago.** It was another 2000 years before the first alphabet appeared. #0486

The world's oldest known scientific **CALCULATOR** was made around **100 BC.** #0487

Around 2110 BC, King Ur-Nammu of Ur became the first ruler to **WRITE DOWN THE LAWS OF HIS LAND** in a written code. There were 57 laws. #0488

Around 500 BC, King Darius, ruler of the Persian Empire, built a **royal road** to a capital city over **2,500 kilometres away.** On foot, the journey would take at least 90 days. #0489

10 STAR-SPANGLED FACTS ABOUT THE USA

The USA was **declared independent from Britain** on 4 July 1776. #0490

Up to 19 presidents have had **attempts on their lives** while in office and four have died **natural deaths.** #0491

The American national anthem is called **'The Star Spangled Banner'.** #0492

Due to unusual circumstances, two **unelected men** were running the USA between 1974 and 1976. #0493

The term **'First Lady'** for a president's wife comes from President Zachary Taylor in 1849, when he used it for his late wife at her funeral. #0494

Four USA presidents – Lincoln, Garfield, McKinley and Kennedy – were **assassinated**. #0495

Eight of the first nine **presidents** were British, because they were born before the country became independent! #0496

The government met in eight different cities before settling on **Washington DC** as the USA capital in 1790. #0497

Before joining the USA, the states of **Vermont, Texas and Hawaii** were all independent republics with their own governments. #0498

Grover Cleveland is the only president to serve **two non-consecutive terms,** so he is both the 22nd and the 24th president. #0499

The **NAZCA** people of South America cut **HUNDREDS OF SHAPES** of animals, birds, trees and flowers into the desert between AD 400 and 650, some as big as 270 metres across.

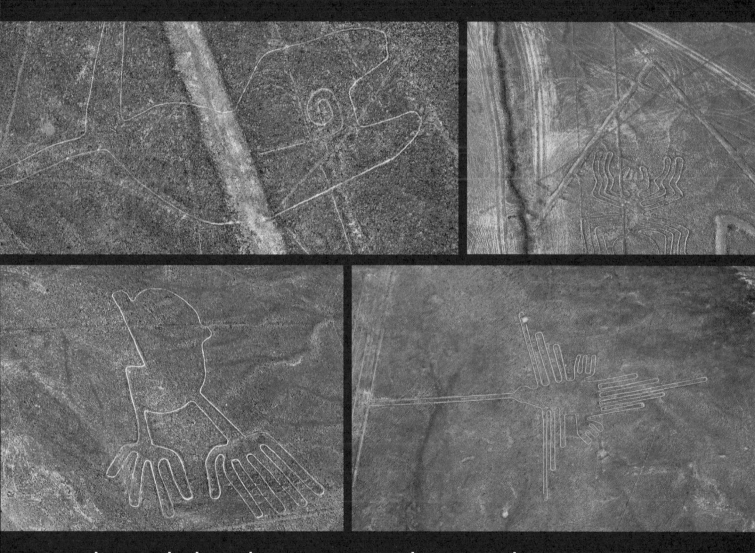

As they didn't have aeroplanes, they would **NEVER HAVE KNOWN** what they really looked like. #0500

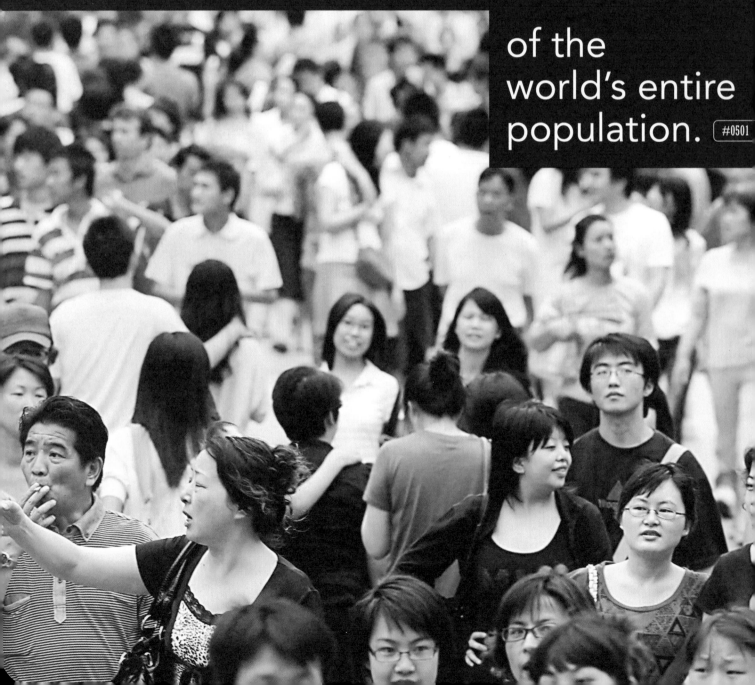

As of December 2011, **CHINA** is the **MOST POPULATED COUNTRY IN THE WORLD,** with almost **20%** of the world's entire population. #0501

SOCIETY AND CULTURE SHOCKERS

The world's longest tunnel is the Thirlmere Aqueduct, a 155-kilometre water tunnel under the north of England. #0502

10 POPULAR FACTS ABOUT POPULATIONS

The world's **population** is over **7 billion** and rising fast. #0503

In **1960,** the population of the world was **3 billion** people. #0504

During 2011, about **135 million** people were born in the world... #0505

The world's population is increasing by **2.4 people a second.** #0512

... and **57 million** died. That's an increase of 78 million people in just one year. #0506

252 babies are born in the world every minute, or **4.2 births a second.** #0511

107 people die in the world every minute, or **1.8 deaths a second.** #0507

The highest life expectancy in the world is in Japan – **83 years.** #0510

More than **60%** of the world's population live in **Asia.** #0509

On 29 May 2007, for the first time in human history, more people lived in **cities and towns** than in the countryside! #0508

10 TONGUE-TWISTING FACTS ON LANGUAGES

The most commonly spoken language in the world is **Mandarin Chinese,** spoken by **845 million people.** #0513

The United Nations recognizes **six official world languages:** Mandarin Chinese, Spanish, English, Arabic, Russian and French. #0514

Around the world, people speak about **6,500 different languages.** #0515

Approximately 83 of these are spoken by **80% of the world's population.** #0516

Approximately 473 of the world's languages are **almost extinct** and spoken only by a few people. #0517

Approximately one language dies out in the world **every two weeks,** when its last speaker dies. #0518

The **Sumerian language** of the Middle East is one of the earliest on record, dating back to around **2900 BC.** #0519

Most **European languages** are closely related to each other, such as German and Dutch. #0520

However, **Euskara,** the language of the Basque people in northern Spain, is **unrelated to any other known language** in the world. #0521

In 1825, blind Frenchman **Louis Braille** developed a language that could be read by blind people by feeling a series of bumps on paper. #0522

3 BOREDOM-BUSTING BOOK FACTS

The world's **longest novel** is Marcel Proust's *A la recherche du temps perdu* (In Search of Lost Time), which has more than **1.5 million words** and was originally published in seven volumes. #0523

The **oldest printed book** is the Diamond Sutra, a Buddhist religious text printed in China in AD 868. #0524

In 1969, the French writer Georges Perec wrote *La Disparition* (The Void) **without using the letter 'e'.** He followed that up in 1972 with *Les Revenentes* (The Ghosts) in which **'e' is the only vowel used.** #0525

The **Victoria Cross** is the highest British military decoration, awarded for bravery. #0526

First given by Queen Victoria in 1857, the Victoria Cross has been awarded **1,357 times.** #0527

The **Purple Heart** is awarded to US servicemen or women wounded or killed in service. #0528

US presidents have awarded almost **2 million** Purple Hearts. #0529

The **Freedom Award** from the International Rescue Committee is for extraordinary contributions to the cause of refugees and human freedom. #0530

The **Turner Prize** is an annual visual arts prize in the UK. In 1999, Tracy Emin's controversial shortlisted piece featured an unmade, messy bed! #0531

The highest award in Denmark is called the **Order of the Elephant,** usually given to heads of state and members of the royal family. #0532

The **'British Order of the Bath'** gets its name from the old ceremony of ritually bathing a new knight to purify him. #0533

Swedish inventor **Alfred Nobel** left money in his will for international prizes for peace, chemistry, physics, medicine, economics and literature. #0534

Nobel Prizes bring prestige for winners – and a small fortune! In 2012, each prize was worth around **£700,000.** #0535

3 FASCINATING FACTS ABOUT WORLD RELIGIONS

There are around **2.5 billion Christians** in the world today, around one third of the world's population, making Christianity the most popular religion in the world. #0536

One of the world's oldest and smallest religions is Samaritanism, practised by around 500 people in Israel and Palestine. #0537

The **Zoroastrian** religion began around 1200 BC and was the main religion of the Persian Empire – and the world – during the 500s BC. Now it has fewer than 200,000 followers worldwide. #0538

33 CRAZY CULTURAL FACTS

Nine countries in the world have **nuclear weapons.** #0539

15 countries, including Costa Rica, have **no military forces.** #0540

There are about **1.4 million men and women** on active duty in the US military. #0541

Russia is the **largest country,** covering over 17 million square kilometres, or **13% of the world's land area.** #0542

The world's smallest country is the **Vatican City in Rome.** It covers 0.44 square kilometres, or around 62 football pitches. #0543

The coral islands of the Maldives in the Indian Ocean peek out of the sea at a **maximum height** of **2.4 metres.** #0544

Tibet is the **highest region** in the world, at a height of 4,900 metres above sea level. #0545

The border between Canada and the United States is the **longest international border** between two countries, at **8,891 kilometres.** #0546

Most countries have a coastline, but **48 are landlocked**, which means citizens have to pass through another country to get to the sea. #0547

Nearly 18,000 people pack into every square kilometre of the principality of Monaco, the world's **most densely populated country.** #0548

There are only **1.7 people for every square kilometre** of Mongolia, the world's emptiest country. #0549

Japan has the oldest population, with nearly a quarter of people aged over 65. #0550

The Burj Khalifa building in Dubai is nearly 830 metres tall, or **over 100 stacked houses.** #0551

Disabled athletes have a long history of competing in the Olympic Games. An American gymnast competed in 1904 with one leg, and a one-armed Hungarian took part in shooting events in 1948 and 1952. #0552

The UK pound sterling is the **oldest currency still in use.** The silver penny was introduced around 1,300 years ago. #0553

Paper money was first used in China in 1024. #0554

It is believed that the **first coins** were produced in Aegina in Greece in around **700 BC.** #0555

In 1946 the Hungarian national bank issued a banknote for **100 quintillion (100 million million million)** pengo. #0556

Somalia issued a coin **in the shape of a guitar.** #0557

There are **150 billion US 1 cent coins** in circulation. #0558

If all the US 1 cent coins in circulation were piled up they would stand **232,500 kilometres** high, or three-fifths of the way to the Moon. #0559

Each US 1 cent coin loses money, as they cost **2.4 cents to make** and distribute. #0560

If you counted one US 1 cent coin every second it would take **4,757 years to complete counting.** #0561

Some people have unusual beauty rituals including **teeth sharpening, ear elongations, nose studs and lip plates.** #0562

The **world's oldest international organization** was set up in Britain in 1839 to campaign for the abolition of slavery. It is now called Anti-Slavery International. #0563

The United Nations was formed in 1945 to promote **world peace**. It has **193 members.** #0564

The Red Cross was set up in 1863 after a Swiss businessman witnessed the wounded lying on a battlefield and was appalled at the lack of medical care. #0565

The idea for the **Scouts** came during a war in South Africa in 1899–1902. **Robert Baden-Powell** was so impressed with the young cadets who ran errands that he founded the Scouts when he got home. #0566

The **Academy Award Oscar** statue is modelled on Mexican film director and actor Emilio Fernandez. #0567

James Cameron directed the two highest-earning movies of all time, *Avatar* and *Titanic*. Combined, they have made over **£2 billion at the box office.** #0568

If the figures for the highest-earning film were adjusted to allow for price rises since release, *Gone With the Wind* from 1939 would be **the most successful.** #0569

The longest film ever made is *Modern Times Forever*, which runs for **10 days.** #0570

The **first feature film with dialogue and music** was *The Jazz Singer*, a 1927 musical. #0571

More copies of the **BIBLE** are **SHOPLIFTED** than of any other book. #0572

10 MIND-BENDING FACTS ABOUT GOVERNMENTS

Elizabeth II of the UK is also queen of **16 Commonwealth countries,** including Canada, Australia, New Zealand and Jamaica. #0573

The current **longest-serving head of state,** King Rama IX of Thailand, has been in power since 1946. #0574

The current **oldest head of state** is Robert Mugabe, who was born in 1924. #0575

No king or queen has entered the **UK House of Commons** since 1642... #0576

... when Charles I stormed in with his soldiers and **tried to arrest** five members of Parliament. #0577

Of all the countries in the world, 44 are monarchies, including 16 Commonwealth nations. #0578

The **biggest democracy** in the world is India. **714 million people** were eligible to vote in the Indian general election of 2009. #0579

A **theocracy** is a system of government based on religion – the head of state is selected by a religious group. #0580

There are two theocracies – the **Vatican City** in Rome, home of the Roman Catholic Church, and **Iran,** an Islamic republic. #0581

In **Australia** it is compulsory for citizens over the age of 18 to vote. #0582

5 FLAG-WAVING FACTS

The world's **FIRST FLAGS** were used in ancient China to represent different parts of the army. #0583

The **ROMAN CAVALRY** carried a square flag known as a **VEXILLUM,** from which we get the term vexillology – the study of flags. #0584

The **OLDEST NATIONAL FLAG** in use is Denmark's white cross on a red background, which is nearly 800 years old. #0585

There is no significance to the **12 YELLOW STARS** that appear on the blue **EUROPEAN UNION** flag – the stars just make a neat circle! #0586

The **UNION FLAG OF THE UK** also appears on **29** other national, provincial, state and territory flags around the world, including the Australian national flag. #0587

4 CURIOUS FACTS ABOUT CITIES

14 countries, including Chile, Bolivia and the Netherlands, have **two capital cities.** One state, South Africa, has **three** capitals! #0588

16 COUNTRIES have capital cities of the same or very similar name, including Kuwait (Kuwait), Mexico (Mexico City), Brazil (Brasilia) and Tunisia (Tunis). #0589

The **highest capital city** in the world is **La Paz,** the administrative capital of Bolivia in South America. It stands 3,640 metres above sea level. #0590

At the moment, **Shanghai** in China is the world's most populated city proper, with over 17 million people. #0591

Havergal Brian's Symphony No 1, 'The Gothic Symphony', is the **LARGEST ORCHESTRAL PIECE OF MUSIC** ever written. It needs:

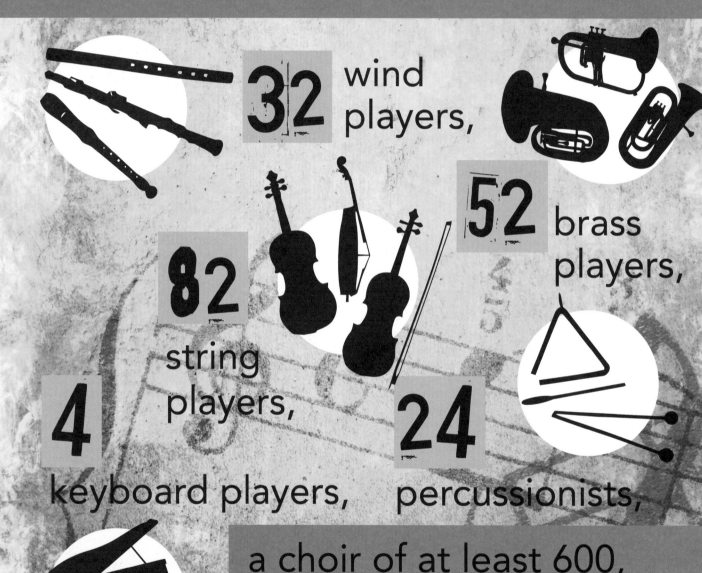

32 wind players,

52 brass players,

82 string players,

4 keyboard players,

24 percussionists,

a choir of at least 600, a children's choir of 100 and four soloists. #0592

10 TOE-TAPPING MUSICAL FACTS

The **best-selling pop single** of all time is 'White Christmas', released by Bing Crosby in 1942. #0593

The **best-selling album** of all time is 'Thriller', released by Michael Jackson in 1982. #0594

In May 2009, more than 100,000 Hindus formed the **biggest choir ever** assembled, in Hyderabad, India. #0595

The **saxophone** is named after its inventor, Adolphe Sax, and the **sousaphone** is named after the American composer John Philip Sousa. #0596

The earliest evidence for the existence of **bagpipes** is in ancient engravings dating back to **1300 BC.** #0597

Wolfgang Amadeus Mozart, born in Austria in 1756, started composing at just **five years old!** #0598

Bagpipes arrived in Scotland in the 1300s and developed into the highland pipes we recognize today. #0599

On the US Billboard chart, the **Beatles** hold the record for **the most Number One hit singles at 20.** #0600

John Cage composed 4'33" in 1952. Instruments play **no notes at all** during its four-minute, 33-second length! #0601

George Beauchamp designed the **first electric guitar** prototype in 1931. It was nicknamed the 'Frying Pan' because of its shape! #0602

10 LUDICROUS FACTS ABOUT LAWS

In the UK, it's an **act of treason** to place a postage stamp of the Queen's head upside down. #0603

In France, it is forbidden to call a pig **Napoleon.** #0604

In Singapore, **chewing gum** is banned. #0605

In Florida in the USA, it is illegal to **skateboard** in a police station. #0606

In the UK, the head of any **dead whale** found on the coast is legally the property of the king; the tail belongs to the queen. #0607

In London, it is illegal to **flag down a taxi** if you have the **plague.** #0608

In Alabama in the USA, it's illegal to be **blindfolded** while driving a vehicle. #0609

In Eraclea in Italy, it is forbidden to build **sandcastles.** #0610

In Vermont in the USA, women must obtain written permission from their husbands to wear **false teeth.** #0611

In Switzerland, it's illegal to **flush a toilet** in a flat after 10pm. #0612

3 FACTS ABOUT EYE-POPPING PRICES

The world's most expensive camera sold for a record-breaking **£1.74 million!** It was one of only 25 made in 1923. #0613

Napoleon Bonaparte's sword is one of the top selling antiques on record. It sold for over **£4 million.** #0614

In 1969, the actor Richard Burton paid **£700,000** for a pear-shaped diamond to give to his wife, Elizabeth Taylor. It has since been resold for about **£3.2 million.** #0615

10 SPORTING FACTS TO EXERCISE YOUR BRAIN

The **oldest sporting event** is the Newmarket Town Plate horse race, run almost every year since 1665. #0616

The **most popular sport** is football. Around 3.3 billion people watch or play the game. #0617

The **biggest ever football crowd** of nearly 200,000 fans watched the World Cup final between Brazil and Uruguay in Rio de Janeiro in 1950. #0618

The World Cup football competition has been held **19 times** since it started in 1930. #0619

More than **2 million people** lined the streets of Madrid to welcome home the winning Spanish World Cup football team in 2010. #0620

Around **15 million people** watch the Tour de France cycle race each year. #0621

Up to **400,000 people** watch the annual Indianapolis 500 motor race in the USA. #0622

Formula 1 racing cars can reach speeds of up to **350 kilometres per hour!** #0623

In 1661, the **first yacht race** took place on the River Thames between King Charles II and his brother, the Duke of York. #0624

Ever since 2000, competitors have taken part in the annual **Mobile Phone Throwing** World Championship! #0625

In **TIBET,** it is considered **POLITE** to **STICK OUT YOUR TONGUE** at your guests. Imagine if you tried that at home! #0626

Chapter 5

THE WONDERS OF

PLANET EARTH

In 1883, the eruption of a **VOLCANO** in Indonesia produced the **WORLD'S LOUDEST-EVER BANG,** which was heard in Australia, 4800 kilometres away. #0627

Steamboat Geyser in Wyoming, USA, shoots jets of scalding water

In 1975, a cricket umpire was struck by lightning that **fused an iron joint** in his leg. #0629

90
metres
into the air. #0628

The springs of Beppu, Japan, are so hot that people have used them to **boil eggs!** #0630

10 LAVA-LICIOUS FACTS ABOUT VOLCANOES

In 1815, the eruption of **Mount Tambora** in Indonesia spread an ash cloud around the world. #0631

Llullaillaco in the Atacama Desert is the **tallest active volcano in the world,** at 6,739 metres! #0632

In 1943, a new volcano in Mexico reached **five storeys high in a week** – Mount Paricutin is now 2,800 metres tall. #0633

The eruption of **Vesuvius** in Italy in AD 79 perfectly preserved the Roman city of Pompeii under a layer of ash – it lay buried for 1,700 years. #0634

Red-hot **lava** flows like sticky liquid. #0635

An eruption on the Caribbean island of Martinique in 1902 killed **almost everyone in the island's capital** – only a few survived. #0637

Over 60% of all volcanoes erupt **underwater.** #0636

Mauna Loa on Hawaii has erupted roughly **every six years since** 1000 BC. #0638

In 1985, an eruption in South America buried the town of Armero under **5 metres of mud.** #0639

In 1952, a Japanese ship, the *Kaiyo Maru*, sank when an **undersea volcano** erupted just below it. #0640

4 INTERESTING ISLAND FACTS

The volcanic island of Surtsey rose from the Atlantic Ocean in 1963, making it the **world's youngest island.** #0641

The **WORLD'S MOST REMOTE ISLAND,** Bouvet Island, is 1,500 kilometres from the nearest landmass, Antarctica. It would take a speedboat travelling at top speed nearly a day to reach it from Antarctica. #0642

The **world's smallest island** is Bishop Rock off the coast of Cornwall – it's just a rock with a lighthouse! #0644

Greenland is the **WORLD'S LARGEST ISLAND.** Australia is three times larger, but it is considered a continent. #0643

5 MASSIVE FACTS ABOUT MOUNTAINS

Mount Everest is the **WORLD'S HIGHEST MOUNTAIN** but Mauna Kea, Hawaii, rises higher from the ocean floor. #0645

The Himalayas contains all of the world's highest mountains, including **100 PEAKS OVER 7,000 METRES TALL.** They are still rising by 0.5 cm a year. #0646

Over **4,000 PEOPLE** have stood on the summit of Everest since the mountain was conquered in 1953. #0647

However, over **200 PEOPLE** have died trying to climb Everest. #0648

When Mount St Helens blew its top in 1980, the volcano lost **400 METRES** from its height. #0649

In 1940, a tornado disturbed a hoard of **BURIED TREASURE,** raining gold coins on a Russian town. #0650

4 COOL FACTS ABOUT THE COAST

The Hawaiian island of Molokai has the **world's highest sea cliffs,** plunging 1,010 metres into the sea – the height of 20 Nelson's Columns. #0651

In 1999, a USA lighthouse was **moved 1 kilometre inland** to save it from toppling into the sea. #0653

The **GREAT BARRIER REEF** runs for **2,600 KILOMETRES** off eastern Australia and is so huge it can be seen from space. #0652

If all the world's coastlines were joined up, they would stretch over **850,000 KILOMETRES.** It would take a speedboat racing at top speed over a year to cruise past. #0654

10 WATERY OCEAN WONDERS

The Atlantic Ocean is getting **4 centimetres wider each year!** #0655

The Mariana Trench in the Pacific is **Earth's deepest point** – so deep, it could submerge Mount Everest. #0656

The Pacific is Earth's deepest ocean, with an average depth of **4,200 metres.** #0657

The Pacific Ocean has more than **25,000 islands.** #0658

Seawater freezes at a **lower temperature** than freshwater, at -1.9°C. #0659

In 1933, a US Navy ship caught in a Pacific storm survived a **34-metre high wave** – the biggest wave at sea ever recorded. #0660

The world's **longest mountain range** is called the mid-ocean ridge – it spans 65,000 kilometres around the globe. #0661

The water in a wave doesn't travel forwards like you might think, it goes **round in a circle.** #0662

If you could remove all the **salt** from the oceans, it would cover Earth's dry land to a depth of **1.5 metres.** #0663

In 1900, 6,000 people died when the town of **Galveston, USA,** was swamped by waves. #0664

The **Amazon River** carries more water than the next eight biggest rivers combined. #0665

Lake Nyos in West Africa, which lies in the crater of an inactive volcano, once released a cloud of **poisonous volcanic gas** that killed 1,700 people. #0666

The Iguazu Falls in South America consists of **275 waterfalls** along 2.7 kilometres of the Iguazu River. #0667

In Alaska, USA, in 1964, **BUILDINGS SANK INTO THE GROUND** when an earthquake caused solid ground to turn to **LIQUID MUD.** #0668

The **world's deadliest earthquake** hit central China in 1556, killing 830,000 people. #0669

Nine out of ten earthquakes strike around the shores of the Pacific Ocean. #0670

Tsunamis (giant waves set off by earthquakes) can race across the ocean at **600 kilometres** per hour. #0671

In 1755, the Portuguese city of **Lisbon** was totally destroyed by an earthquake, fire and tidal waves. #0672

In 1896, Japanese sailors out at sea hardly noticed a tsunami that went on to kill **28,000 people** on land. #0673

The Indonesian earthquake of 2004 released **more energy** than all of the earthquakes in the previous five years combined. #0674

Often, before a tsunami strikes, all the **water drains away** from the shore, exposing the seabed. #0675

An earthquake in 1812 was so strong, it caused the Mississippi River to **flow backwards.** #0676

In 1985, a **healthy baby** was found in a ruined hospital in Mexico City seven days after an earthquake destroyed the city. #0677

In 1976, scientists noticed animals behaving oddly in a Chinese city. The city was **evacuated** and two hours later an earthquake struck. #0678

4 CLEVER CAVE FACTS

Stalactites are rocky needles hanging from cave ceilings, formed by dripping water. The **WORLD'S LONGEST STALACTITE** is 8.2 metres long, in The White Chamber in Lebanon. #0680

Krubera Cave in Georgia, western Asia, is the **deepest known cave,** plunging deeper than 2,000 metres. It would take you about 30 seconds to fall that far! #0679

Mammoth Cave in Kentucky, USA, is the **WORLD'S LARGEST CAVE SYSTEM,** with over 628 kilometres of linked caves and passages. #0681

The **longest underwater cave** found so far is a **215-kilometre maze** of flooded passages in Mexico. It's not yet been fully explored. #0682

5 WINDING FACTS ABOUT RIVERS

The area of land that contributes water to a river is called a 'basin'. The basin of the Amazon River covers **NEARLY HALF OF SOUTH AMERICA!** #0683

The Amazon empties so much water into the Atlantic that freshwater can be found **180 KILOMETRES OUT TO SEA.** #0684

A huge underground river runs under the **NILE,** containing **SIX TIMES MORE WATER** than the Nile itself. #0685

The **WORLD'S SHORTEST RIVER** is the Roe River in Montana, USA, which is only 61 metres long – half the length of a football pitch. #0686

The Yellow River in China is the **WORLD'S MUDDIEST RIVER,** dumping over a billion tonnes of silt into the sea each year. #0687

10 HURRICANE AND TORNADO FACTS TO BLOW YOUR MIND

Hurricanes are huge spinning storms with winds of over **120 kilometres per hour!** #0688

Tornadoes are much smaller than hurricanes, but with winds **three times as strong.** #0689

Hurricanes spin **clockwise** south of the Equator and **anti-clockwise** north of the Equator. #0690

A tornado in Italy sucked a **baby** out of his pram, carried him **90 metres** and set him down safely. #0691

A tornado in England plucked all of the **feathers** off hens in a coop. #0692

Waterspouts whipped up by hurricanes at sea can tower over **100 metres.** #0693

In 1928, a hurricane dumped over **2.5 billion tonnes of seawater** on the Caribbean island of Puerto Rico. #0694

In 1992, a hurricane shifted a **whole island** closer to the US coast! #0695

A hurricane unleashes the same amount of energy as a **nuclear bomb.** #0696

A US tornado lifted a **train off the tracks** and dumped it **25 metres** away. #0697

Six thousand years ago, the **SAHARA DESERT** was lush and leafy, enjoyed by the hippos, giraffes and elephants that lived there. #0698

5 ELECTRIFYING THUNDER AND LIGHTNING FACTS

A bolt of lightning heats the air around it to **30,000°C** – five times hotter than the surface of the Sun. #0699

Lightning travels downwards at **220,000 KILOMETRES PER HOUR** and even faster upwards. #0700

Right now, there are about **2,000 THUNDERSTORMS** raging around the world. #0701

Lightning is very dangerous – it **KILLS AND INJURES** more people each year than hurricanes or tornadoes. #0702

People in the town of Tororo in East Africa hear thunder about **250 DAYS A YEAR.** #0703

The temperature rises around  **30°C** **FOR EVERY KILOMETRE** you travel towards the centre of Earth. #0704

Vast **underground lakes** lie beneath some of Earth's greatest deserts, including the Sahara. Some of the water is being tapped for farming and cities. #0705

At the centre of a raging hurricane is a calm area called the **eye,** where there is very little wind. #0706

All snowflakes have **six sides** but no two that have ever been studied are exactly alike. #0707

In 1881, a violent storm rained **crabs and sea snails** on an English town over 60 kilometres from the coast. #0708

In 1934, a **371-kilometre-per-hour** gust of wind was recorded at Mount Washington, USA! #0709

Snowflakes measuring **38 centimetres,** larger than dinner plates, have fallen in Montana, USA. #0710

In 1986, hailstones the size of **grapefruits** fell on a town in Bangladesh, killing 92 people. #0711

If all the moisture in the air fell as rain, it would cover Earth's surface to a depth of **2.5 centimetres.** #0712

The town of Calama in the Atacama Desert had had no rain for **400 years,** until a shower in 1972. #0713

By the time you've read this sentence, over **900 million tons of rain** will have fallen around Earth. #0714

In 1882, two **frozen frogs** were found inside hailstones in Iowa, USA. #0715

Commonwealth Bay in Antarctica occasionally experiences winds of **320 kilometres per hour.** #0716

The Earth acts like a **GIANT MAGNET** because of its core of molten metal. That's why compasses point north. #0717

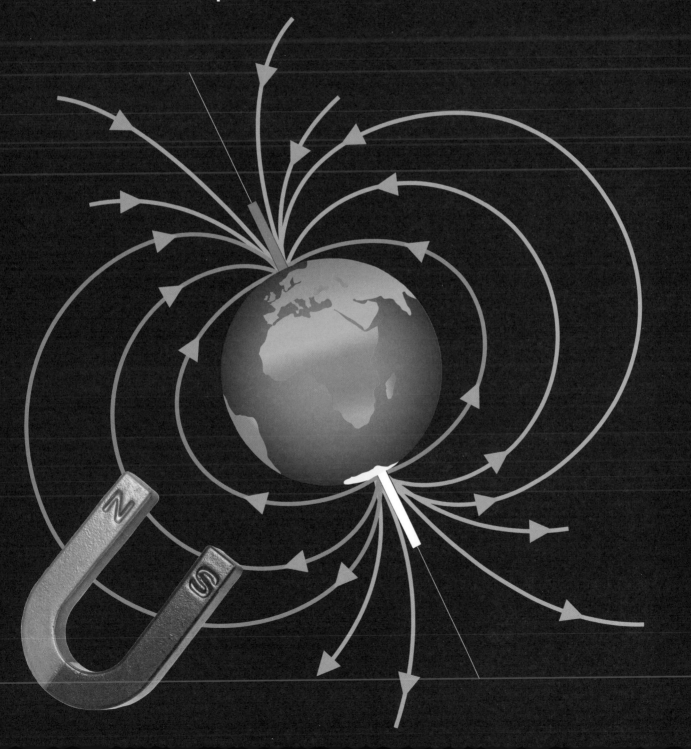

The **world's largest swamp,** the Pantanal in Brazil, covers an area larger than England. #0718

The vast **Ganges Delta** in Asia, a swampy area where two mighty rivers meet, covers an area the size of Scotland and Wales. #0719

The **Great Rift Valley** is a **6,000-kilometre trench** that has been created where two of the giant plates that make up Earth's crust are pulling apart. #0720

Earth's deepest mine is TauTona Goldmine in South Africa, 3,900 metres deep. #0721

The **deepest hole ever bored**, Kola Borehole in Russia, descends 12,200 metres! #0722

All the gold mined in a year would fit inside the **average living room.** #0723

The **largest gold nugget** ever found is the 'Welcome Stranger', found in 1869 in Australia. #0724

The **first diamond found in South Africa** was picked up by children on a beach. #0725

The world's **largest diamond,** the Cullinan Diamond, was the size of a large egg. #0726

The **world's most valuable gem** is painite, a small crystal found only in Burma. #0727

Earth's oldest fossils are 3.4 billion years old. #0728

The **world's largest pearl,** the Pearl of Lao Tzu, is about the same size as a football. #0729

Only **one in a thousand oysters** contains a **pearl.** #0730

5 DRAMATIC FACTS ABOUT DESERTS

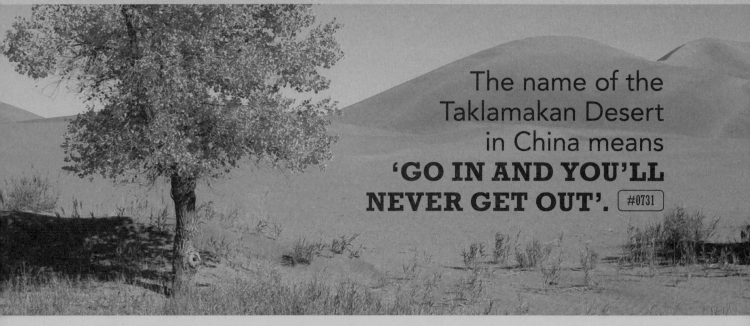

The name of the Taklamakan Desert in China means **'GO IN AND YOU'LL NEVER GET OUT'.** #0731

The Sahara Desert, **EARTH'S BIGGEST DESERT,** covers an area about the size of the United States. #0732

It is still getting bigger – growing **50 KILOMETRES** south every year. #0733

Despite being covered in ice, **ANTARCTICA** is actually classed as a desert because it hardly ever snows! #0734

In 1913, the temperature at Furnace Creek in Death Valley, USA, hit a sizzling **56°C** – the highest on record in the country. #0735

4 EARTH-SHATTERING EARTHQUAKE AND AVALANCHE FACTS

In 1970, an **earthquake** in Peru triggered an avalanche that buried the town of Yungay and its 20,000 inhabitants. #0736

A cliff collapse in northern England in 1993 sent a **HOTEL TUMBLING INTO THE SEA.** #0737

The cliffs of Holderness in Britain are moving **1 TO 2 METRES INLAND** each year as they are eaten away by the sea. #0738

In 1916, **avalanches** in the Alps killed 10,000 soldiers fighting in World War I. #0739

10 SPARKLING ICE FACTS

Antarctica holds **70% of Earth's freshwater,** locked up in ice. #0740

The largest iceberg ever seen was the size of **Jamaica!** It broke off Antarctica. #0741

The **tallest iceberg** ever spotted was a 167-metre whopper floating off Greenland. #0742

The Sahara Desert was covered by **glaciers** 450 million years ago. #0743

In 1991, the **5,000-year-old** preserved body of a huntsman was found in a glacier in the Alps. #0744

In 1848, ice blocked **Niagara Falls** for nearly two days, so people explored the dry river bed. #0745

In 1912, 1,502 people died in icy waters when an **iceberg** sank the 'unsinkable' ship, *Titanic*. #0746

In 1829, a chunk of ice weighing 2 kilograms **inexplicably fell** on the town of Cordoba in Spain. #0747

If all the ice in Antarctica melted, sea levels would rise by **67 metres!** #0748

The South Pole is covered by a sheet of ice **2,700 metres** thick. #0749

In 1859, a shower of fish fell on Glamorgan in Wales when a strong updraught of wind sucked them out of the sea and dropped them inland. #0750

Chapter 6

SCIENCE AND

TECHNOLOGY AND BRAINBUSTERS

Humans share about **HALF OF THEIR DNA** with a banana. #0751

The water you drink was once **DRUNK BY DINOSAURS** – it's recycled again and again. #0752

Apollo 11, the spaceflight that took astronauts to the moon in 1969, had less computing power than a **modern mobile phone.** #0753

The Arab inventor al-Jazari made the **first robots** around AD 1200! #0754

In the 1830s, Charles Babbage designed the **first computer printer** but it was not built until 2000. #0755

3D computer printers **'print' solid objects,** building up the design layer by layer from plastic. #0756

The power of computers **doubles** roughly every two years! #0757

The **first personal computer**, Altair 8000, was launched in 1975. #0758

It had no screen, no keyboard, no disk drive, no mouse and had to be **built from a kit.** #0759

45 robots of 14 'species' live in Robotarium X, a **robot zoo** in Portugal. #0760

The **first webcam** showed the coffee pot in a university computer lab, to tell workers when the coffee was ready. #0761

There are around **17 billion devices** connected to the Internet – more than two for every person on Earth. #0762

10 CRAZY COMPUTER FACTS

10 MIND-BOGGLING MATHS FACTS

If you put a single **grain of rice** on the first square of a chessboard, then two on the next square, then four, and kept on **doubling** the rice, for the last square you would need enough rice to cover India to a depth of 1 metre. #0763

The Pirahã tribe in Brazil have words for only 'one', 'two' and 'many' so can't count **three or more objects.** #0764

Our system of 60 seconds in a minute and 60 minutes in an hour comes from the **Babylonian counting system** devised 4000 years ago. #0765

$12 + 3 - 4 + 5 + 67 + 8 + 9 = 100$
and
$1 + 2 + 34 - 5 + 67 - 8 + 9 = 100$.
There are at least nine more sums like this. #0766

You can turn a strip of paper into a **shape with only one surface** by twisting it once and gluing the ends together. #0767

There is an infinite number of infinities. **1, 2, 3...; -1, -2, -3...; 0.1, 0.11, 0.111...; 0.1, 0.12, 0.13...; 0.1, 0.01, 0.001...** #0768

A **googol** is 10^{100}, which is 1 followed by 100 zeroes. This is **larger than any number that needs to be counted.** #0769

A **googolplex** is 10^{googol}. It would take longer than the universe has existed (around 13 billion years) to write this number out in full. #0770

The pattern of seeds in a sunflower head, the shape of a nautilus seashell and the arrangement of leaves around a plant all follow the same spiral pattern, called the **golden spiral.** #0771

The mathematician Descartes invented the system we use for drawing graphs, using X- and Y-axes, after watching a **fly crawl over the ceiling** as he lay in bed. #0772

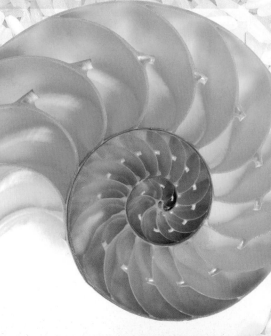

More than

99.9%

of all species
of plants
and animals
that have
ever existed
are now
EXTINCT. #0773

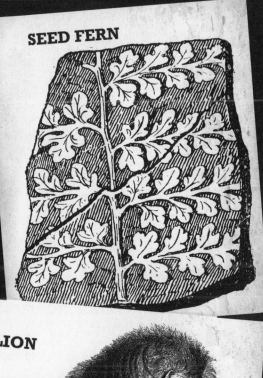

SEED FERN

CAPE LION

TASMANIAN
WOLF

DODO

5 TRULY EXTREME EXPERIMENTS

Sir Isaac Newton poked a **LARGE, BLUNT NEEDLE** into his eye to test his ideas about optics (the properties of light). #0774

Italian priest Lazzaro Spallanzani swallowed **TINY BAGS OF FOOD** attached to threads and pulled them up from his stomach after a few hours to find out how food is digested. #0775

A study in 2009 found that cows who have been given names **PRODUCE MORE MILK** than unnamed cows. #0776

By crushing lumps of amber (made from tree resin) scientists can capture tiny puffs of the atmosphere **THE DINOSAURS BREATHED.** #0777

Stubbins Ffirth, a trainee doctor, tried to show **YELLOW FEVER CANNOT BE PASSED BETWEEN PEOPLE** – he dripped vomit from fever patients into cuts on his arms, into his eyes and even swallowed it. (Although he lived, he was wrong – yellow fever is contagious!) #0778

DAISY

3 GOBSMACKING ENVIRONMENTAL FACTS

Recycling one aluminium can can save enough electricity to power a TV for three hours and aluminium cans can be recycled an unlimited number of times. #0779

At least **20 million hectares of rainforest** are lost every year, which is as big as England, Scotland and Wales combined. #0780

The **next ice age** is due to start in about 1,500 years, but might be delayed by climate change. #0781

A laser is a beam of light energy. Some lasers are so concentrated they can vaporize a bulldozer **1,800 METRES AWAY.** #0782

Velcro was invented in 1948 after a scientist found burs (sticky seeds) stuck to his dog's fur. (Under a microscope he saw they had tiny hooks.) #0783

The **wasabi fire alarm** releases the smell of wasabi, a strong-smelling horseradish, to warn deaf people of fire. #0784

Canned food has been around since 1772, but the **can opener** wasn't invented until 1855. #0785

In 1996, an American man invented a portable, zip-up cage to hide inside to escape an attack by **killer bees.** #0786

In 2007, an American woman invented a bra that converts into two **emergency gas masks.** #0787

Sir Francis Bacon invented **frozen chicken** in 1626, but he died from a chill he caught experimenting with his method for freezing the chicken. #0788

Barcodes were designed in 1949 by Norman Woodland drawing in sand at the beach. He extended the dots and dashes of Morse code into bands. #0789

The **first submarine,** the *Turtle,* used glow-in-the-dark mushrooms to provide light. #0790

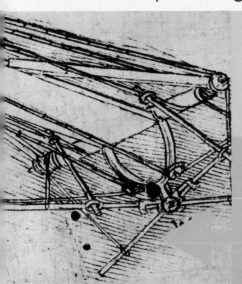

The designers of the **CD** decided it must be able to hold Beethoven's Ninth Symphony at any tempo – so CDs hold **72 minutes of music.** #0791

Leonardo da Vinci, who died in 1519, drew designs for a **tank,** a **helicopter,** a **submarine** and a **parachute.** #0792

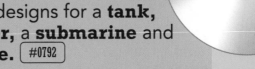

149

35 FACTS ABOUT
SCIENCE & TECHNOLOGY

Electricity travels as fast as the speed of light, about **300,000 kilometres per second.** #0793

One 60-watt light bulb is the equivalent of about **25,000 fireflies.** #0794

An electric eel can produce an **electric shock** of 500 volts - enough to kill an adult. #0795

Gregor Mendel, a scientist in the 1800s, came up with ideas on **genetics** (how traits are passed from one generation to the next) by looking at **pea pods and their flowers.** #0796

The **smallest flowering plant** is *Wolffia angusta*. It would fit inside this letter 'o'. #0797

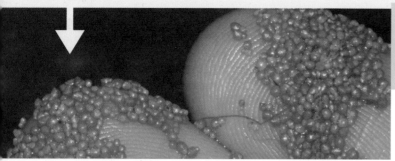

The 'desert onion' onyanga grows in the Namib Desert in Angola. It can live for up to **2,000 years.** #0798

A mushroom called 'Lady in the veil' can be heard **cracking as it grows** by a centimetre a minute. #0799

African bugleweed contains a chemical that messes up caterpillars so they turn into **butterflies with two heads.** #0800

The largest unit of measurement for distance is a **gigaparsec**, about **3.26 billion light years** or **31,000 trillion kilometres.** #0801

The **Scoville heat unit (SHU)** is used to measure the **heat of chillies.** #0802

Horsepower is used to measure the **power of engines.** It began when people running steam-powered vehicles paid a fee based on the number of horses they had been saved from using. #0803

The **number of atoms** in the whole universe is thought to be around 10^{80}. This is **1 followed by 80 zeros.** #0804

Most of every atom is **empty space.** Each atom has a **nucleus with electrons whizzing around it** — if the nucleus was the size of a basketball, the electrons would be **32 kilometres away.** #0805

If you took all the **space out of atoms**, the whole human race would be **the size of a sugar cube.** #0806

Atoms are very tiny — about **25,000,000,000,000,000,000,000 carbon atoms** make up the lead of a pencil. #0807

The **oldest known rock** is in Canada and is **4 billion** years old. #0808

There are **bacteria that live in the spaces between crystals** inside rocks. #0809

Sound travels **ten times faster** through rock than air. #0810

Although **rubies are red and sapphires are blue**, they are the same rock – impurities make them **different colours**. #0811

The temperature at the Earth's core is **over 5,500°C.** #0812

The **magnetic field** of the Earth reverses **four or five times every million years**, with the North and South Poles swapping over. #0813

Scientists collect ice up to **800,000 years old** in Antarctica and from bubbles in it they can **sample the ancient atmosphere.** #0814

India was once an island and the Himalayas formed when it slowly crashed into Asia, **pushing the edges of each landmass upwards.** #0815

Fossils of marine animals are found on Mount Everest and in the Himalayas, as the land that forms them was **once under the sea.** #0816

Since 1977 the unmanned **spaceships Voyagers 1 and 2** have been carrying a message for any **aliens they meet.** #0817

The USSR put an **unmanned lander on Venus** in 1970. The USA has still not landed a craft on the planet. #0818

The temperature on the surface of the Sun is over **5,500°C.** #0819

If you could convert the heat energy from a space shuttle's rocket boosters to electric power, **two minutes would supply the power needed by 87,000 homes** for a day. #0820

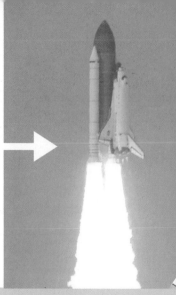

The spacecraft **Rosetta weighed 100 kilograms on Earth**, but when it landed on a comet low gravity **reduced its weight to that of a sheet of paper.** #0821

There are 170,000 kilograms of **human junk on the Moon**, including **two golf balls** left by an astronaut. #0822

Americans make up **5% of the world's population** but use **25% of the world's energy.** #0823

A beam of sunlight usually appears **white**, but is actually made up of different colours. If the beam hits raindrops at the right angle, **the colours separate and we see them as a rainbow.** #0824

The iceberg that sank the *Titanic* was made from snow that fell over Greenland **3,000 years ago.** #0825

A microbe known as **'strain 121'** lives in holes under the sea that pour out water at **temperatures of 121°C** – much hotter than boiling water. #0826

Nothing can be colder than **zero Kelvin (-273°C).** #0827

10 TERRIFIC TRANSPORT FACTS

A **Boeing 747** travels **800 metres** on each litre of fuel. As it can carry 550 passengers, it's more fuel efficient than most cars. #0828

Early airships were filled with hydrogen, a highly flammable gas. After some deadly explosions, helium was used instead. #0829

The **longest train** in the world was 7,350 metres long. It had eight engines and 682 wagons! #0830

The **earliest known successful flight** was by hot air balloon in Paris in 1783. #0831

The word **'juggernaut',** a huge lorry, is Indian – it's the name of a Hindu temple cart said to be used to crush people. #0832

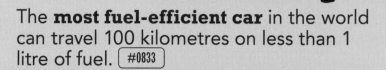

The **most fuel-efficient car** in the world can travel 100 kilometres on less than 1 litre of fuel. #0833

Maglev trains have **no wheels** – they are suspended above a rail by magnetic force. #0834

In 1972, Jean Boulet landed a helicopter safely after the **engine failed** at a height of 12,440 metres. #0835

The South American Aztecs didn't make use of the **wheel,** so didn't have carts or carriages. Instead they travelled and transported things via canoe. #0836

There will be around **200,000** aeroplane flights in the world today. #0837

The **GREAT PACIFIC GARBAGE PATCH** is a floating mass of around 110 million tonnes of plastic waste and chemical sludge that has collected in the Pacific Ocean. #0838

When you're **sitting still,** you're actually **moving!** #0839

That's because Earth rotates at **1,670 kilometres per hour** and moves around the Sun at **107,280 kilometres per hour.** #0840

Then the solar system moves at **70,000 kilometres per hour** through the galaxy, and the galaxy spins at **792,000 kilometres per hour.** #0841

10 FANTASTIC FACTS ABOUT FORCES

When you jump, you exert a **tiny force on Earth,** shifting it very slightly in space. #0842

Light doesn't always travel in straight lines – it can be bent by gravity, so it curves around planets and stars. #0843

Pigeons navigate using special brain cells that detect the strength and direction of magnetic fields. #0844

A full bottle **breaks more easily** than an empty bottle. #0845

A **feather** and a **bowling ball** dropped at the same time on the **Moon** would reach the ground together. #0846

Every object has **its own gravity.** #0847

A ship trapped in a **freezing sea** would be crushed by the force of ice forming around it. #0848

Sledges move over **water,** not snow. Heat from **friction** melts a layer of snow and the sledge glides over. #0849

If you break a **magnet** in half, each half will instantly get its own north and south poles. #0850

Planet Earth would be the size of a **marble** if it had the same gravity as a black hole. #0851

10 UNSTABLE FACTS ABOUT CHEMICALS

Mercury is the only metal which is a **liquid** at room temperature. #0852

Polonium-214 lasts less than a fifth of a second before half of it has changed into lead. #0853

98% of the normal matter in the universe is **hydrogen** and **helium.** #0854

Stars crush together **hydrogen** and **helium** under huge pressure, making all other chemical elements. #0855

In 2006, scientists developed a material that could one day be used to make **invisibility cloaks!** #0856

Common salt is made of sodium and chlorine, both of which are dangerous to humans on their own. #0857

In 2008, scientists in Mexico discovered a way of making tiny **diamonds from tequila,** by heating it to 800°C. #0858

Oobleck is a paste of water and cornflour. If you slap it hard it feels almost solid, but if you put your hand into it slowly it is liquid. #0859

Berkelium, a silvery-white radioactive metal, is the rarest element on Earth. Only 1 gram has been made since 1967. #0860

Super-alloys are made by adding a tiny amount of one metal to another. #0861

4 EARTH-SHAKING DINOSAUR FACTS

The ferocious **Tyrannosaurus rex** might have been covered with fluffy **feathers!** Lots of dinosaurs were feathered. #0862

Dinosaurs ruled the Earth for more than **TWICE AS LONG** as they have been extinct. #0863

A baby pterodactyl is called a **'flapling'**. #0864

Microraptor was only 60 centimetres long. It was covered with feathers and had four wings instead of arms and legs. #0865

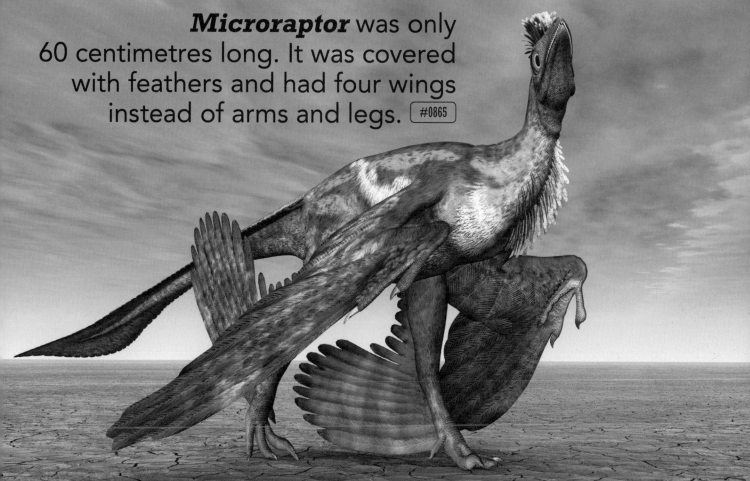

10 FACTS ON THE HISTORY OF SCIENCE

Early doctors put **maggots** into wounds to eat decaying flesh, helping the wounds to heal. #0866

The Ancient Greeks thought a camel mating with a leopard produced the **giraffe!** #0867

2,600 years ago, Buddhist philosophers suggested that all matter is made of **atoms.** Modern physics has reached the same conclusion. #0868

Centuries ago, doctors in India would let an **ant** bite through the edges of a wound then snap off its head, leaving the jaws to act as a stitch. #0869

The first important **dinosaur fossils** were found by a 12-year-old girl, Mary Anning, in 1811 in Dorset, England. #0870

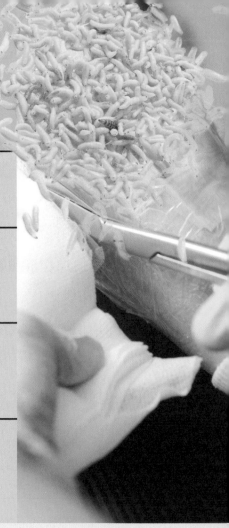

In 1947, an American engineer invented the **first microwave,** which was nearly 2 metres tall! #0871

Scientist Robert Bunsen suffered **partial paralysis** and **lost an eye** in an explosion in 1840 when he was researching toxic and explosive compounds called cacodyls. #0872

In 1746, a scientist sent an electric charge along **1,500 metres of wire,** held by 200 monks. All the monks yelled at the same time, showing electricity moves very quickly! #0873

The **giant squid** was thought to be legendary until it was photographed in 2004. #0874

A scientist trying to extract **gold from urine** discovered **phosphorus** by mistake in 1669. #0875

Forensic science can be used to help solve criminal cases. In the case of **FORENSIC ENTOMOLOGY,** scientists examine insects found in and around human remains to determine the time of death, or even if the body has been moved! #0876

Chapter 7

EXPLORING SPACE

The **SUN** is so huge, **1.3** million Earths would fit inside it.

#0877

Planet Earth is not **perfectly round,** but actually bulges in the middle. #0878

A satellite uses very little energy – about as much as **two ordinary light bulbs.** #0879

A rocket needs to travel at **40,000 kilometres per hour** to escape Earth's gravity. #0880

162

10 GLOWING FACTS ABOUT THE MOON

Human footprints on the Moon will last for **millions of years,** because there is no wind to blow them away. #0881

The largest crater on the Moon is the South Pole-Aitken basin, almost **2,414 kilometres across!** #0882

There are **no noises on the Moon,** because there is no air to carry sounds. #0883

As there was no wind, the American flag planted on the Moon by astronauts was **held straight with wire.** #0884

Only **12 people** have walked on the surface of the Moon. No one has been there since 1972. #0885

The Moon is moving away from Earth at the rate of **3 centimetres a year.** #0886

Moonlight takes **1.25 seconds** to reach Earth. #0887

We only ever see **one side of the Moon** from Earth. #0888

Temperatures on the dark side of the Moon fall to **-173°C!** #0889

Most scientists believe the Moon formed when a **collision** broke off a chunk of Earth. #0890

would **FLOAT ON WATER.** #0891

5 HOT FACTS ABOUT THE SUN

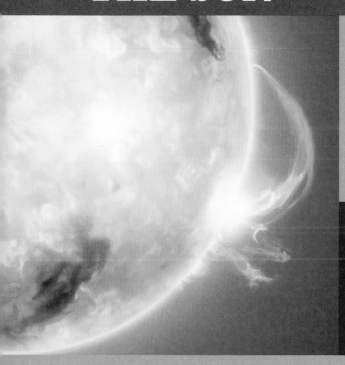

Sunlight takes **EIGHT AND A HALF MINUTES** to reach Earth, travelling at 300,000 kilometres per second. #0892

Fountains of flame **LARGER THAN EARTH** shoot from the surface of the Sun. #0893

Dark spots on the Sun called **SUNSPOTS** can measure 80,000 kilometres across – larger than the planet Uranus. #0894

The temperature at the centre of the Sun is **150,000 TIMES HOTTER** than boiling water. #0895

The Sun contains **99.8%** of all the matter in the solar system. #0896

Mercury's atmosphere is so thin that if all of it was collected it wouldn't fill a **party balloon.**
#0897

Mercury and Venus are the only planets that have **no moons.** #0898

The weight of Venus's atmosphere would **crush you instantly.** #0899

A **day** on Venus lasts longer than its **year.** #0900

Venus is called **'Earth's evil twin',** because it is a similar size but hostile to life. #0901

Olympus Mons on Mars is the **tallest volcano in the solar system.** It stands three times the height of Mount Everest. #0902

The surface of Mars is icy-cold, with temperatures that rarely rise above **freezing,** even in summer. #0903

The Grand Canyon on Mars is **twenty times wider** than the Grand Canyon in Arizona, USA. #0904

Earth is the **only planet** we know of in our solar system that humans can live on. #0905

About **71%** of Earth's surface is covered by water. #0906

The **longest eclipse of the Sun** lasts no more than seven and a half minutes. #0907

Stars are **different colours** depending on how hot they are. The hottest stars are blue, medium ones like our Sun are yellow, cooler stars are red. #0908

In space, **blood rushes to your head,** making your face appear puffy. #0909

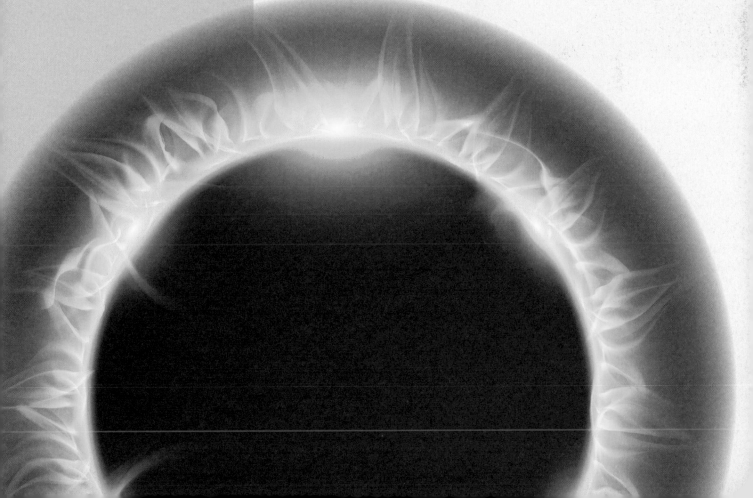

4 FACTS ABOUT CRAZY COMETS

COMETS speed up as they approach the Sun, to over **1.6 MILLION KILOMETRES PER HOUR.** #0910

A **comet** is a ball of ice and dust. As it shoots through space a comet's tail always points away from the Sun. #0911

The longest comet tails are over **10 MILLION KILOMETRES LONG,** resembling a streak of light across the sky. #0912

Halley's Comet appears every **76 years.** It will next be seen in 2061. #0913

5 FACTS TO ROCK THE GALAXY

Scientists believe there are over **100 BILLION GALAXIES** in the universe. `#0914`

The galaxy nearest to our own is the **ANDROMEDA GALAXY.** Starlight from this galaxy takes 2 million years to reach us. `#0915`

The Milky Way and Andromeda Galaxy may collide in about **5 BILLION YEARS' TIME** to form one huge galaxy. `#0916`

All the stars in a galaxy are held together by **GRAVITY.** `#0917`

The Milky Way is estimated to be around **13.2 BILLION YEARS OLD.** `#0918`

Your skin would **inflate like a balloon** if you entered space without a spacesuit. #0919

Saturn's famous rings are made of **millions of chunks of rock and ice.** #0920

The Sun is about **halfway** through its 10 billion-year lifetime. #0921

10 WOW FACTS ABOUT OUTER PLANETS

Jupiter spins **faster than any other planet.** A day there only lasts about ten hours. #0922

The giant Red Spot on Jupiter is a **whirling storm** that has been raging for at least 300 years. #0923

Jupiter is **so huge** that all the other planets in the solar system would **fit inside it.** #0924

Jupiter has the **most moons** of any planet – at least 63. #0925

There are a total of seven rings, made up of **millions of ice crystals,** orbiting around Saturn. #0926

Saturn is the **lightest planet** in the solar system – it is mostly made up of hydrogen and helium. #0927

Seasons last over **20 years** on the planet Uranus. #0928

Uranus is **tilted on its side** so one of its poles always faces the Sun. #0929

Neptune has howling winds **ten times stronger** than those on Earth. #0930

Neptune's moon, Triton, is one of the **coldest places in the solar system**, with a temperature of -235°C. #0931

5 SECRETS OF THE UNIVERSE

In 2012, a British space scientist used a special maths equation called the **DRAKE EQUATION** to predict that we have four intelligent alien civilizations in our galaxy. #0932

Instead of 'little green men', the scientist also predicts that they may look like **FOOTBALL-FIELD SIZED JELLYFISH,** with onion-shaped limbs and an orange underbelly! #0933

In 2011, astronomers discovered a star that they believe is composed **ENTIRELY OF DIAMOND.** It measures 60,000 kilometres across – five times the size of Earth. #0934

Earth may have **FOUR MORE MOONS.** In 1986, a scientist discovered an asteroid in orbit around the Sun that appeared to be following Earth. Since then, at least three similar asteroids have been discovered. #0935

Earth is **NOT FLAT** – but **THE UNIVERSE MIGHT BE!** Using Einstein's Theory of General Relativity and scientific measurements, scientists believe it is. #0936

The things we know – planets, stars, galaxies, black holes – make up just **4%** of the Universe.

The rest is unknown stuff – **23% DARK MATTER** and **73% DARK ENERGY** that scientists still can't really explain. #0937

10 SMASHING FACTS ABOUT METEORS

Over a **million meteors** (shooting stars) will burn up in Earth's atmosphere today. #0938

Rock from a **meteorite** sells for as much as gold. #0939

A meteorite that fell 65 million years ago probably caused the **extinction of the dinosaurs.** #0940

Some scientists believe **life arrived on Earth** on a meteorite. #0941

Asteroids are **giant space rocks.** The largest, Ceres, is 950 kilometres across. #0942

Over **40,000 shooting stars** fell in 20 minutes during a meteor shower in 1966. #0943

In 1954, an American woman was seriously injured when a meteorite **crashed through her roof.** #0944

An **Egyptian dog was killed** when it was struck by a meteorite in 1911. #0945

In 1908, a meteorite broke up, causing a **gigantic fireball** that flattened 80 million trees. #0946

Earth is **getting heavier each year,** because of the meteorites and other space debris that crash here. #0947

4 LOST FACTS ABOUT BLACK HOLES

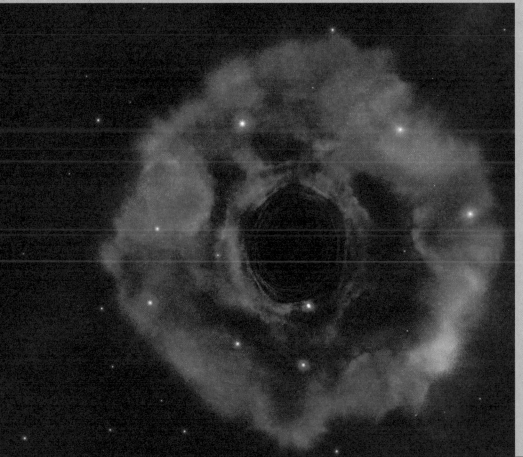

A black hole is born when a dying star collapses in an **EXPLOSION** called a **SUPERNOVA.** #0948

A black hole **sucks everything nearby into it.** Nothing can escape from a black hole, not even light. #0949

In a black hole, **time virtually stops.** That's because time goes more slowly as gravity increases. #0950

If you fell into a black hole your **BODY** would be **STRETCHED LIKE SPAGHETTI.** #0951

The **LARGEST METEORITE EVER FOUND** fell in Namibia, southern Africa, in 1920. It weighed over **60** tonnes – as much as **15 ELEPHANTS.**

Distances between stars are measured in **light years** (the distance light travels in a year – about 10 trillion kilometres). #0953

Stars called **supergiants** are 70 times larger than our Sun. #0954

Our nearest star, Proxima Centauri, is 4.3 light years away – about 40 trillion kilometres. #0955

The brightest stars in the Milky Way shine 5 million times brighter than the Sun. #0956

In 1974, scientists searching for life on other planets beamed a message at a group of stars. It will take **25,000 years** for the message to arrive and **50,000 years for any reply.** #0957

A rocket travelling at the speed of the Apollo spacecraft would take **900,000 years** to reach Proxima Centauri. #0958

Stars appear to **twinkle** because of varying air currents in Earth's atmosphere. #0959

Our galaxy, the Milky Way, contains at least **100,000 million stars.** #0960

The Milky Way is shaped like a spinning **Catherine wheel firework.** #0961

Many stars come in **pairs.** Planets orbiting twin suns have two sets of sunsets and sunrises. #0962

10 SHINING STAR FACTS

4 FACTS ABOUT ANIMAL ASTRONAUTS

In 1957, a Russian dog named Laika became **the first animal to orbit Earth.** Unfortunately, Laika did not survive her trip. #0963

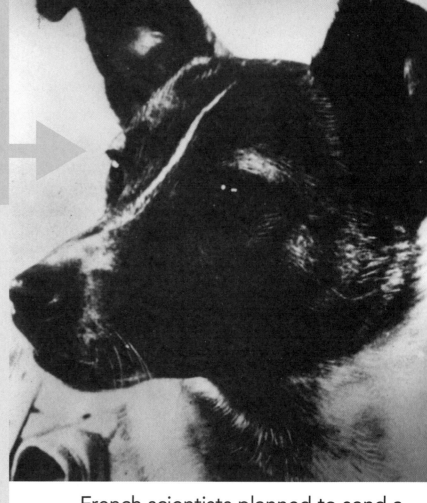

Animals that have travelled in space include **mice, a rabbit, a frog and a tortoise.** #0964

French scientists planned to send a **CAT CALLED FELIX** into space in 1963, but he escaped. A replacement, Félicette, made the trip instead. #0965

The **first monkey in space** was called Albert II. Albert I sadly died before he got to take a trip. #0966

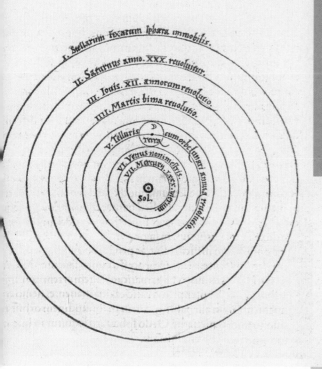

5 FACTS ABOUT EARLY IDEAS OF SPACE

In around 260 BC, Greek astronomer Aristarchus of Samos suggested the Sun was **THE CENTRE OF THE SOLAR SYSTEM.** It took 1,800 years to prove he was right. #0967

In the 1600s, you could be **THROWN IN PRISON** or even **TORTURED** for suggesting Earth was not the centre of the solar system. #0968

In 1543, astronomer Nicolaus Copernicus claimed the planets **MOVED AROUND THE SUN.** His book was banned until 1835. #0969

People believed the skies were unchanging until sixteenth-century astronomer Tycho Brahe noticed a **NEW STAR IN THE SKY.** #0970

The word **COMET** comes from the Greek, for 'long-haired', as they were once thought to be **LONG-HAIRED STARS.** #0971

The Apollo spacecrafts took three days to reach the Moon.

At this speed it would take a rocket

96 YEARS

to reach the planet Neptune, the most distant planet in the solar system.

#0972

10 FACTS ABOUT SPACE EXPLORERS

The **first man-made object to orbit Earth** was a Soviet satellite called Sputnik in 1957. [#0973]

Soviet cosmonaut Valentina Tereshkova became the **first woman in space** in 1963. [#0974]

In 1961, Soviet cosmonaut Yuri Gagarin became the **first man in space.** [#0975]

On 20 July 1969, the Americans landed **the first man on the Moon.** [#0976]

Neil Armstrong was the **first man to walk** on the Moon's surface, but Buzz Aldrin took the first pee on it. [#0977]

In 1970, the crew of Apollo 13 **nearly died** when an oxygen tank explosion crippled their craft. [#0978]

In 1986, space shuttle Challenger **exploded** seconds after takeoff. [#0979]

The American Moon landing programme cost **£16 billion** – the cost today would be around £93 billion. [#0980]

In 2012, the American probe Voyager 1 became the **first man-made object** to leave the solar system. It was launched in 1977. [#0981]

The rocks collected from the Moon by the Apollo astronauts weigh a total of **382 kilograms.** [#0982]

Venus is surrounded by clouds of poisonous **sulphuric acid.** #0983

There may be up to **100,000 million comets** orbiting the Sun. #0984

Neptune is the **stormiest planet** in the solar system. #0985

4 SPACE-TASTIC INVENTIONS

Smoke detectors were used on a space station in the 1970s. #0986

Silvery **SPACE BLANKETS** used by marathon runners were invented when 1960s scientists discovered that metal film used in satellites kept people warm. #0987

The **CORDLESS DRILL** was first invented to gather rock samples on the Moon. #0988

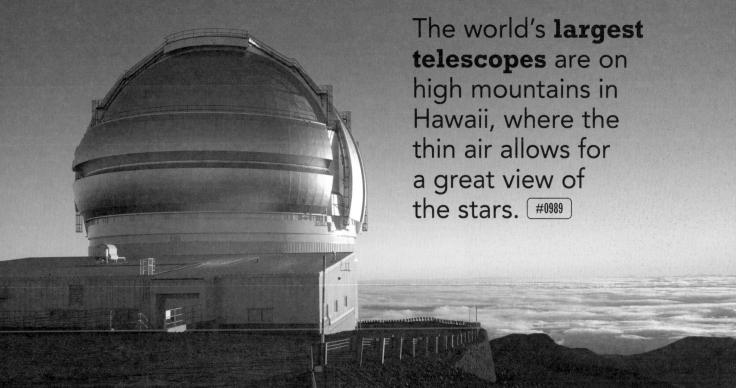

The world's **largest telescopes** are on high mountains in Hawaii, where the thin air allows for a great view of the stars. #0989

10 FACTS ABOUT LIFE IN SPACE

Russian cosmonaut Sergei Krikalev has spent **over two years** of his life in space. #0990

You get a little taller in space because there is **no gravity** to squash your bones. #0991

Astronauts living in space exercise for at least **two hours** each day so their muscles don't waste away. #0992

When in space, astronauts have to **strap themselves onto the toilet!** #0993

When they go to the toilet, a **vacuum cleaner** is used to suck up waste. #0994

Astronauts on board space shuttles saw **16 sunrises** and **16 sunsets** a day because the shuttles orbited Earth 16 times in 24 hours. #0995

It takes a day to prepare for a **walk in space,** to allow the body to get used to the environment. #0996

Space-walking astronauts wear **adult-size nappies.** #0997

Astronauts use the **Vomit Comet,** which simulates weightlessness and encourages nausea, to prepare for zero gravity. #0998

The **Olympic torch** once flew on a space shuttle. #0999

TELESCOPES are a bit like TIME MACHINES.

The most powerful telescopes can look back in time, seeing stars as they were millions of years ago. #1000

INDEX

ACKNOWLEDGEMENTS

t = top, b = bottom, l = left, r = right, m = middle

Cover images iStockphoto and Shutterstock.com
Other images courtesy of Dreamstime.com,
iStockphoto, Getty Images and Shutterstock.com.

Getty Images
8tr Visuals Unlimited, Inc./Ken Catania/Getty Images, 19t Barcroft
Media/Getty Images, 31 Tier Und Naturfotografie J und C Sohns/
Getty Images, 53 FilmMagic/Getty Images, 88r SSPL/Getty Images,
121b Planet Observer/Getty Images, 135m Tsuneo Yamashita/
Getty Images, 143 Time & Life Pictures/Getty Images, 153 AFP/
Getty Images, 158b Carrie Vonderhaar/Ocean Futures Society/
Getty Images, 178 Getty Images, 181mr Getty Images, 181b
Michael Dunning/Getty Images.

Shutterstock.com
9 Stanislaw Tokarski/Shutterstock.com, 13 Dmitry Berkut/
Shutterstock.com, 21 Chris Mole/Shutterstock.com, 54 Jamie
Roach/Shutterstock.com, 71 Phil64/Shutterstock.com, 87
FeatureflAsh/Shutterstock.com, 89 Kiev.Victor/Shutterstock.com,
90 Bocman1973/Shutterstock.com, 94–95 Tonyv3112/Shutterstock.
com, 101 Kobby Dagan/Shutterstock.com, 109 Nicku/Shutterstock.
com, 110 Andy Lidstone/Shutterstock.com, 112 Rob Wilson/
Shutterstock.com.

20 Sandstein/Creative Commons Attribution

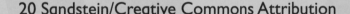

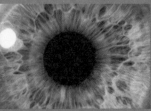
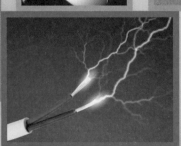